Win Her with Dinner

Food, Booze, and Tunes
for Cooking Up the Perfect Evening

Doug Veith   Tom Greenwood   Alex Hilebronner

RODALE

© 2004 by Doug Veith, Tom Greenwood, and Alex Hilebronner

Photographs © by Ryan McVay/Getty Images (pepper mill), John A. Rizzo/Getty Images (vegetable peeler), Mitch Mandel & Kurt Wilson/Rodale Images (all other kitchen equipment), Photodisc Collection/Getty Images (compact disc), Catherine Ledner/Getty Images (cow), G. K. & Vikki Hart/Getty Images (chicken), James Worrell Photography, Ltd./Stock Food (fish), Solzberg Studio/Stock Food (asparagus), Grant Symon/Getty Images (cherries)

The quote on page 15 is reprinted with the permission of Simon and Schuster Adult Publishing Group from *Parker's Wine Buyer's Guide, Fourth Edition*, by Robert M. Parker Jr. Copyright © 1995 by Robert M. Parker Jr.

Book design by Tara Long

Library of Congress Cataloging-in-Publication Data

Veith, Doug.
Win her with dinner : food, booze, & tunes for cooking up the perfect evening / Doug Veith, Tom Greenwood, Alex Hilebronner.
     p.   cm.
Includes index.
ISBN 1-57954-797-4 hardcover
1. Dinners and dining.   2. Cookery for two.   I. Greenwood, Tom.   II. Hilebronner, Alex.
III. Title.
TX737.V45   2004
641.5'612—dc22
                                                                      2003022733

Distributed to the book trade by St. Martin's Press

2 4 6 8 10 9 7 5 3 1   hardcover

WE INSPIRE AND ENABLE PEOPLE TO IMPROVE THEIR LIVES AND THE WORLD AROUND THEM

FOR MORE OF OUR PRODUCTS
WWW.RODALESTORE.COM
(800) 848-4735

Contents

Acknowledgments   v

Behind the Food   1

Equipment, Basic Ingredients, and Utensils   3

Should Do's and Shouldn't Do's   9

Drink This   13

Play This   17

Red Meat
Steak, Potatoes, Green Beans, and Salad   28
Steak and Potatoes with Spinach
    and Shrimp   32
Beef-Asparagus Stir-Fry with Rice
    and Soybeans   36
Veal with Pasta and Asparagus   40
Lamb Chops, Veggies, and Salad   44
Steak Tacos, Black Beans, and Chips
    with Salsa   48

White Meat
Chicken, Veggies, and Salad   54
Chicken-and-Veggie Stir-Fry with Rice   58
Pork, Cornmeal Mush, and Tomatoes   62
Chicken, Couscous, Zucchini, and Salad   66
Turkey, Green Beans, Salad, and Bread   71
Pork Chops, Green Beans, Salad,
    and Bread   76

Sea Meat
Tuna, Rice, Veggies, and Cucumber Salad   82
Salmon, Couscous, Peas, and Salad   86
Lobster, Asparagus, Potatoes, and Bread   90
Shrimp Tacos, Rice, Beans, and Zucchini   94
Sole, Mini-Broccoli, Rice, and Toast   99
Swordfish, Veggies, Potatoes, and Toast   104

No Meat
Tomato-Basil Pasta, Salad, and Toast   110
Pasta with Veggies, Salad, and Bread   114
Pasta and Mushrooms, with Salad and Bread   118
Ravioli, Asparagus, and Bread   122
Creamy Yellow Rice, Asparagus, Salad,
    and Bread   126
Rice-and-Bean Tacos with Corn   130

Desserts
Fresh Strawberries with Sour Cream
    & Brown Sugar   138
Lemon Tarts with Fresh Blueberries   139
Lemon & Berry Sorbet with Fresh Raspberries   140
Three Flavors of Japanese Mochi Ice Cream   141
Vanilla Bean Ice Cream with Kahlúa,
    Hot Fudge, Chocolate-Covered
    Espresso Beans, & Whipped Cream   142
Warm Apple Tarts with Vanilla Ice Cream   143

Aftermath   145

Index   147

Acknowledgments

The authors would like to thank:

Ben Affleck

Base Design

John Carter

Geoff Cook

Matt Damon

Brian DeFiore

Ian Ehling

Dave Freeman

The Greenwood Family

Catherine Hilebronner

Jean Jones

Jennifer Landers

Kathryn C. LeSage

Catherine McCord

Scott Mosier

Paula Pister

Darra Rochelle

Jan Schrader

Jennifer Smith

Kevin Smith

Barbara Veith

Carolyn and Dick Veith

Ben Young

"For guys like me, who can't cook a lick, this book is a godsend—particularly since it turns out that cooking appears to be something that matters to women. If you're completely hapless (like me), you'll find this book the easiest and best guide to making a wonderful meal."
—Ben Affleck

"For ordinary guys looking for an alternative to the generic dinner date. This is the type of thing you pick up and say, 'I wish I'd thought of that.' A clever concept fully realized—and highly entertaining to boot."
—Matt Damon

"If you're looking to win a woman's heart, stomach, and other goodies, this book is an absolute must. Follow these recipes to the letter and you'll definitely add a few notches to your bedpost."
—film director Kevin Smith

"Laugh your way through this witty book. Then cook your way through the dinner date of your life. Fabulous food and drinks, great music to listen to, even a few grace notes to spice up your dinner conversation—this gem's got it all. Well, everything but the girl."
—David Joachim, author of *Fresh Choices* and the *New York Times* bestseller *A Man, a Can, a Grill*

Behind the Food

Picture this: a candlelit dinner with the woman of your dreams in the comfort of your own home. The two of you wash down a mouthwatering spinach-portobello fusilli with the perfect bottle of Chianti, while Miles Davis serenades you with his sultry sounds. And—get this—you've orchestrated every detail of this moment all by yourself.

Sound cheesy? Not to women—they eat that stuff up.

All right, so you don't know what fusilli is. And who is this Davis guy? Relax, man. That's why you're holding this book.

One evening several years ago, a few guys, much like you and your friends, got together to hang out, drink beer, and eat something. And drink beer. There was a palpable sense of possibility and purpose in the air. Little did these unsuspecting young men know they were on the verge of making a discovery that would forever alter man's relationship with the kitchen—and man's relationship with woman.

That evening, for reasons lost to history (and beer), the guys decided to actually cook dinner for themselves. A real dinner. What they made is not important. What *is* important is that, being guys, their cumulative "cooking" experience consisted of only ice, microwaved popcorn, and the occasional scrambled egg.

Guided only by primordial instinct and wielding only a couple of dull paring knives and some dented, hand-me-down pans, these culinary cavemen pressed onward, hungry but undaunted. Within a couple of hours, dinner was served. The results of the experiment were surprising to all involved: The food was edible. More than that, it actually tasted good! With that watershed evening, fears of cooking were conquered and a tradition was started.

But the real revelation came as girlfriends were worked into (and, more often than not, back out of) subsequent feasts: Women were seriously impressed! Not necessarily by what these fledgling chefs were cooking but by the simple fact that they were cooking at all. "Seriously impressed" was all these guys needed to hear.

"What?" the men marveled. "Women impressed? With us? For cooking? Hmm . . ." They paused, raised a collective eyebrow, then smiled wide. The seeds of a great idea had been planted.

Flash forward several years and many haircuts to the book you're now clutching in your semi-moist mitts. Its premise is based upon the simple truth that women like to see a guy put forth a little effort. Let's face it, any schmo can take a woman to a swanky restaurant and slap down his credit card. Cooking for a woman, however, immediately puts you ahead of the pack by showing her you've put a dash of initiative, a smidgen of energy, and a pinch of thought into the date.

We recognize that most guys don't cook. It's not that they can't; they just don't. But why is that? Could it be that guys think of the kitchen only as the place where the beer and condiments are kept? Could it be that guys are content to eat just about anything this side of crayons? Could it be that they have relied on their mothers, girlfriends, ex-wives, cafeterias, kwik-e-marts, and pizza joints for sustenance? We know firsthand that it's not one of those things—it's all of those things rolled up into one big thing.

This book is not "Cooking for Morons"; it's simply cooking for guys who are cooking for girls. Unlike other recipe books, it calmly walks guys through the making of not merely individual entrées but entire meals, complete with matching sides and salads. Each simple and simply scrumptious recipe has been guyed down (not dumbed down, mind you) to its essentials and is written in straightforward plain speak that's as easy to swallow and digest as Jell-O.

And seeing as this book is specifically for guys, we've taken nothing for granted and left nothing to chance. Replete with recommendations for wine and music, each recipe is a blueprint for a complete, self-contained, ready-to-share evening, start to finish. But wait, there's more! We've even included tips on etiquette and how to create a comfortable setting without compromising one whisker of your guyhood.

By now you're probably asking yourself, "Who is the 'we' behind this brilliant but simple concept?" "We" is Alex, Doug, and Tom. Alex is a sought-after professional private chef in Los Angeles who has worked for A-list clients (one of whom once demanded she FedEx him meals while he was working in a foreign country). Doug and Tom are professional guys who, not surprisingly, cook like guys. Their guyish inclinations in the kitchen have been tempered and abetted by Alex's culinary expertise and intuition as well as her womanly insight. With *Win Her with Dinner*, the three have teamed up to combat the forces of evil (the worst of those being hunger and loneliness) and to inspire, entertain, and enlighten guys in the kitchen and in their love lives.

So what are you waiting for? Pick up the phone. Give her a call. And cook for her. Who knows, maybe you'll even like it. We know she will.

Equipment, Basic Ingredients, and Utensils

Okay, you're ready to cook for a woman. Or are you? Before you reach for the phone and invite her over for dinner, you need to have a few simple items that are a must for any active *cucina*: some cooking equipment, eating utensils, and a few basic ingredients. Think serviceable cookware, metal silverware, nonpaper/nonplastic tableware, and a few staple foodstuffs besides the soy sauce packets buried under the rubber bands in your kitchen junk drawer.

As far as basic kitchen equipment goes, all of the items we will list are necessary tackle for cooking and are easy to find in most discount, department, or kitchen supply stores. You may already have functional versions of many of these items; you can fill in the gaps by raiding your parents' basement or hitting a local flea market. In general, pick the equipment that best suits your budget.

Same goes for the tableware you will be using to eat and drink. Chances are you have a basic set of these things lying around. Note, however, that plastic sporks and commemorative beer cups from sporting events and spring breaks do not a good impression make. Real plates and silverware are not expensive and will give your cooking a legitimate raison d'être (that's French for "reason to eat"). This is all a part of what foodophiles call *présentation*.

Finally, the pantry primer: Each recipe calls for a few basic ingredients that any nondormant kitchen should stock. These INGREDIENTS YOU SHOULD ALREADY HAVE, as we call them in the recipes, are rudiments of day-to-day cooking. All are inexpensive and have a "no pressure" shelf life. Once you're outfitted with these raw materials, you'll be ready to start cooking other raw materials.

With a little organization and a minimal investment, you will be ready for not only the *Win Her with Dinner* recipes but a whole new life in the kitchen.

Good luck and enjoy.

Kitchen Equipment You Will Need

 · **Stockpot with lid:** This big pot with a handle on each side is good for cooking pasta, making soup, or boiling lobster.

 · **Medium saucepan with lid:** A versatile workhorse, this pot has a long handle and is used for anything from steaming vegetables to boiling potatoes.

 · **Small saucepan with lid:** This mini saucepan is useful for boiling eggs, melting butter, making rice, and reheating small portions of leftovers.

 · **2 large frying pans with lids:** These skillets come in handy for everything from making stir-fries to frying fish to sautéing vegetables to making sauces.

- **Large and small baking pan:** Use these low pans to broil or bake red meat, chicken, fish, and vegetables. Ceramic baking pans are good because they are easy to clean.
- **Baking sheet:** This flat metal cookie sheet is good for making garlic bread, crostini, and cookies.
- **4 mixing bowls:** Many recipes require more than one of these for making marinades, sauces, or toppings. Conveniently, mixing bowls are usually sold in sets, with smaller ones stacked within larger ones.
- **Strainer:** This is good for draining cooked pasta and boiled veggies and for rinsing rice and veggies before cooking. Get one with a fine mesh screen and a handle.
- **Grater:** The flat, handheld type will suffice for grating cheese and ginger.
- **Vegetable peeler:** This not only peels carrots and other veggies but also shaves cheese into bigger pieces than a grater can.
- **Pepper mill:** No kitchen is complete without this—it's a must for spicing up salads, pastas, meats, et cetera with fresh-ground pepper.

- **Chef's knife:** This long, broad, tapered blade is needed for cutting, chopping, slicing, and dicing.
- **Paring knife:** This short blade is handy for when a big chef's knife is too unwieldy.
- **Bread knife:** Its serrated edge is good for slicing or cutting any kind of baked good.
- **Cutting board:** You need this so you don't destroy your countertops. Get one that's big enough to hold a couple of piles of chopped vegetables.
- **Can opener**
- **Measuring cups and spoons:** Get a set for dry ingredients, plus a large 2- or 4-cup liquid measure.
- **Spatula:** This utensil is crucial for flipping and serving food.
- **Wooden spoon:** Keep one on hand for stirring and flipping food and for general cooking.
- **Tongs:** These are helpful for flipping and serving hot food.
- **Whisk:** Use to mix marinades, salad dressings, and sauces.
- **Kitchen scissors:** Keep an extra pair handy for opening plastic packaging, trimming chicken, chopping herbs, cutting open lobster tails, and so on.

- **Timer**
- **Meat thermometer:** This is essential for making sure meat has cooked long enough.
- **2 pot holders:** So you don't burn your hands.
- **Paper towels**
- **Plastic wrap:** Use this to keep food fresh in the fridge.
- **Aluminum foil:** Foil can cover food while it's cooking in the oven.

Basic Ingredients You Will Need for Cooking

These are the staples you should keep in stock. Each recipe will require a few items from this list, designated as **Ingredients You Should Already Have**.

- **Bottle extra virgin olive oil:** The finest of olive oils, those designated extra virgin can be used in everything from salad dressings to marinades and as a general cooking oil.
- **Bottle toasted sesame oil:** Made from sesame seeds, this oil has a nutty taste and is often used in Asian cooking.
- **Butter:** This is available salted or unsalted; we recommend salted because it tends to have a little more flavor.

- **Bottle balsamic vinegar:** This Italian vinegar made from white grapes assumes a dark color because it is aged in wooden barrels. It's often used in salad dressings and marinades. Don't skimp on your balsamic; most supermarket brands are just cheap vinegar with caramel coloring.
- **Bottle red wine vinegar:** This tangy, pinkish vinegar made from red wine is also used in salad dressings and marinades.
- **Bottle soy sauce:** The most common sauce in Asian cooking, this is derived from a combination of fermented soybeans and grains. Varieties range from light (thin and salty) to dark (thick and sweeter).
- **Jar Dijon mustard:** A sharpish, tangy mustard from Dijon, France, this is excellent as a condiment and as an ingredient in salad dressings and marinades.
- **Fresh garlic:** This is used in virtually every type of cuisine in the world.
- **Box salt:** Among the many varieties are iodized table salt, sea salt, and kosher salt. We recommend kosher salt for its coarse grain and subtle taste.
- **Black peppercorns:** The difference between fresh-ground pepper and powdered pepper is like night and day.
- **Bottle finely ground white pepper:** Use white pepper when you want the taste of pepper without the black specks.

Chop Shop

Within this book's recipes, we tell you to do certain things but don't always tell you how. Nearly all of our instructions should be self-explanatory to even the greenest of cooks. For example, "Set the oven to 350°F" is a no-brainer. Likewise, "Place the baking pan on the middle oven rack" should be a can of corn for anyone old enough to read and tall enough to reach the middle rack. But when we tell you to "finely dice the garlic" or "finely chop the onion," well, that's a whole different bulb of stink.

Below, we'll differentiate between "dicing" and "chopping" and bestow upon thee the savoir faire that is required before the dice is cast. Which isn't to say that chopping is all that dicey. In terms of difficulty, dicing and chopping exist in a galaxy far, far away from rocket science. But follow our instructions and you'll most likely emerge from your chopping experience with all of your digits intact. And one last thing: If, for whatever reason, you start to run while holding a knife, keep it point down. That way, you won't stab yourself in the eye—you'll only stab yourself in the quadriceps.

There are two sides to an onion: the stem end (or the "top") and the root end (or the "bottom"). For clarity, the root end contains the bushy dried roots.

1. Place the onion on a cutting board and use a chef's knife to cut a ¼" slice from the stem end.

2. Peel back and remove the outer papery skin.

3. Place the root end on the cutting board. Halve the onion lengthwise, from top to bottom, cutting through the center of the root.

4. Place the two halves cut-side down on the cutting board. For each piece, grip the root end with your noncutting hand to stabilize the piece while you cut. Starting approximately ¼" from the root, make a series of evenly spaced parallel cuts from the bottom end to the top end. (Don't cut all the way through the root; leaving it intact will help hold the slices together. Think of the root as an anchor.) You can control the size of your dice via the spacing in between your parallel slices: Closer together = smaller dice. Farther apart = bigger dice, or chop.

5. Make 3 horizontal cuts into the onion by holding your palm flat and straight on the rounded part of the onion while carefully slicing along the onion in a direction parallel to your hand. Be sure to keep your hand and fingers out of the way!

6. Now it's time to complete your dice, by making evenly spaced, crosswise cuts in the onion, in the opposite direction of the first slices you made—think of a tic-tac-toe board. For a square and precise dice, try to keep your spacing the same as for the first set of slices you made. Voilà—perfectly diced pieces of onion!

Utensils You Will Need for Eating and Drinking

- **4 dinner plates:** The extra dinner plates can double as serving plates.
- **4 small plates:** These should be smaller than dinner plates but bigger than saucers. You'll use them for serving salad, bread, and/or dessert.
- **Salad bowl**
- **4 cereal bowls:** You'll need these for serving dessert and some salads.
- **4 forks**
- **4 knives:** These should be sharp enough to cut meat.
- **4 spoons**

- **2 serving spoons:** Larger spoons are good for tossing and serving salad and other food.
- **4 napkins:** Cloth napkins are recommended.
- **4 wine glasses:** It's always good to have a few extra wine glasses in case of breakage.
- **2 water/beer glasses:** Simple pint glasses will suffice.
- **Corkscrew/wine opener:** A Screwpull corkscrew is foolproof.

Should Do's and Shouldn't Do's

People are finicky about what they will or won't eat, for any number of reasons ranging from legitimate to downright bizarre. So, to avoid any menu mishaps, we propose that you clear your proposed meal with your proposed date ahead of time. In short: Not everyone eats everything, and you don't want to shove food down anyone's throat.

Need further convincing? Just imagine going to the effort of preparing a lamb chop dinner for a woman you didn't know was a militant, card-carrying vegetarian. While that would mean more lamb for you, it would likely also mean you'd be eating alone. Or picture yourself rushing your swollen, itchy date to the emergency room because you were oblivious to her sesame oil allergy. And last but not worst: Visualize cooking up some succulent pork chops for Sharon Foster, only to learn that she was born Sharon Finkelblatz, the daughter of Rabbi Finkelblatz.

Narrowing down your meal options is just the first step in your recipe for success. Here are some other hints for making sure your evening goes smoothly.

Before She Gets There

When you're having a woman over for dinner, a clean home/apartment is of the utmost importance. We really can't stress this enough. If your place looks gross, it probably is gross. And if your place is gross, your guest may conclude that you are gross and that your cooking, therefore, must also be gross. Don't let this happen to you!

So, where to begin making the place presentable? First, check on the condition of the can. Start by thoroughly policing the joint for errant pubes. Slap on some rubber gloves and brush out the hopper using way, way too much powdered cleanser. Scrub off any moss or mushrooms that may have set up shop in your shower. And if your toothbrush looks like you've been using it as a trowel, get rid of it. Have soap and a clean hand towel available by the sink and, while you're there, chip off any petrified toothpaste globules. And be sure to have a full roll of toilet paper cued up—women go through jaw-dropping quantities of that stuff.

As your guest will at some point in the evening check herself out in your bathroom mirror, make sure to wipe off any toothpaste spatter and popped-zit shrapnel. It's also a good idea to take a look in the medicine cabinet and remove any incriminating pharmaceuticals, just in case she gets curious.

Obviously, you should also clean the rest of your living space, but that goes without saying. So why are we saying it? Because you're a guy, and cleanliness is relative: What you consider immaculate may actually register near the bottom end of her cleanliness spectrum.

It should also be said at this point that tidiness and cleanliness, while both obligatory, are two related but totally different things. The former may give the illusion of the latter but is by no means a substitute therefor. Both are necessary evils for the greater good and to avoid the bad and the ugly.

Translation? Take a second to run a damp rag over all flat surfaces to remove the dust tumbleweeds, layers of funk, and sticky rings of whatnot residue that may have snuck up on you since your mom's last visit.

Once your place can pass for clean, you should also make it comfortable. The music should not be too loud, the lighting not too bright. As in the story of the three bears, these elements should be just right. Set the volume of your stereo at a level low enough to be conducive to comfortable conversation but loud enough to drown out that infernal clicking sound you make when you chew. Test your decibel level by acting out a spoken dinnertime scenario with two sock puppets.

Adjust your lighting so it's roughly one-eighth as bright as a Vegas casino yet not so dim that she can't see whether she's got food on her fork. The temperature of your domicile, similarly, should be somewhere between those of a skating rink and an old-folks' home.

If you're in touch with your feminine side, flowers and/or a candle or two can be a romantic touch. Avoid roses; they carry too many implications and can freak women out. Sunflowers are pretty innocuous and are generally masculine as flowers Gogh. If you put candles on the dinner table, avoid the scented kind. Those things can really throw a stink that, when melding with the waft of your dinner, may upset your olfactory orientation.

The bottom line with all of these details is that you shouldn't try to be anything you're not. Except a chef, of course.

Here are a few other adjustments to make before she arrives.

- Take down any photos of old girlfriends. While you're at it, take down any photos that make you look like a moron. Yes, that one, too.
- Hide your porn. We all have a little bit of the smutty smut—and women have an uncanny knack for sniffing it out. So put it in a safe place. Unless, of course, you know that she's into that kind of thing. In which case, make sure to have plenty of it lying around.
- Turn down the volume on your answering machine. Anyone could—and will—call. Your mom. Your boss. A collection agency. Some guy who wants to kick your ass. That old girlfriend whose picture you hid might even call to fill you in on how great her life has been since you broke up. Don't tempt fate.
- Turn off your computer. Especially if you're one of those instant-messaging freaks. Checking game scores and responding to Internet chat partners can surely wait a few hours.

When She Gets There

If she's wearing a coat, help her out of it and then hang it in the closet—the one that the fewest things will fall out of when you open the door. Give her the nickel tour of the place, but don't start with the bedroom. And when you do get to the bedroom, don't say, "This is where the magic happens."

Set her up with a nondairy beverage and make sure she's comfortable. You should also introduce her to any pets you may have, but keep the baby talk and animal speak to a minimum (and hope that she does, too). While you're busy with your duties as host, don't forget about any of your remaining duties as chef.

When Dinner Is Ready

Serve her first, with the plate that looks at least as appetizing as the other. If you burned the food, serve yourself the portion that is "the most well-done." Throughout the evening, keep an eye on her water glass and rehydrate it when it's empty. You may want to ask her before refilling her wine glass, so she doesn't think you're trying to get her loaded. By the way, fill wine glasses half full (or half empty, depending on how you feel the date is going).

Here are a few final manners don'ts.

- Don't salt your food before tasting it, even if you know you're going to salt the crap out of it anyway.
- Don't talk with your mouth full and don't chew with your mouth open. Most important, don't talk with your mouth closed.
- If she excuses herself to go to the restroom, don't offer her a magazine. And don't ask her to leave the toilet seat up when she's finished.
- Don't do the dishes while she's there. You can take care of them next week.
- Don't let her do dishes, even if she insists. Unless, of course, she's bigger than you.
- Don't ask her to do the dishes. Especially if she's bigger than you.
- Don't forget to walk her out at the end of the evening. Provided, of course, she does walk out at the end of the evening.

Drink This

Wine is an important component of any meal, with the possible exception of breakfast. It has the power to set a festive or romantic mood, loosen conversation, enhance your edibles, and turn an ordinary evening into an extraordinary one. Or at the very least, turn an ordinary evening into one so memorable that you can't remember it.

At the most basic level, red wines tend to go well with red meat and dishes with stronger flavors and tomato-based sauces. White wines are generally paired with chicken, seafood, and cream sauces. Pink wines go well with sundresses and sorority happy hours.

These are not hard-and-fast rules, however, and exceptions are many. The bottom line is that a wine should complement and enhance the flavors of your food, not compete with them.

A wine is typically named according to either the type of grape it is predominantly made from or the region that produced its grape(s). For example, merlot, chardonnay, and cabernet sauvignon are types of grapes, whereas Chianti, Chablis, and Rioja are wine-producing regions. The International Commission of Wine Snobbery and Elitism (ICWSE) has established this convoluted system precisely to confuse and alienate folks like us.

The serving temperature of a wine is, mercifully, more straightforward. It's a detail that should not be overlooked as it will directly affect how your wine tastes, not to mention how cold it feels in your mouth. Wines served too cold will be difficult to properly taste and fully appreciate, while wines served too warm will taste flabby and out of balance. And the last thing any of us wants is for our wine to taste flabby and out of balance. Red wines should be served at "cellar temperature" (65° or so—Fahrenheit, dude, not Celsius, not Kelvin). While, technically, a cellar is a room, do not confuse cellar temperature with room temperature. If you don't have a cellar, you can approximate said temperature by tossing your red in the fridge for 20 to 30 minutes or so before serving. Whites should be served only 5° to 10° cooler than reds and can be chilled in the fridge for 45 to 50 minutes prior to pouring. If your date arrives before the temperature of your wine is exactly right, do not attempt to compensate by adding ice or putting wine in the microwave. This will turn your wine into brine.

This may be more information than you need or want. If you're new to Vinoville, you may want to start with the recommendations that we give with each recipe. On the following pages, we offer laymen's descriptions of all those wines below. Or you could just go to your local wine shop and ask the clerk with the comb-over for some help.

We encourage you to experiment and try different wines with different foods. But don't get too crazy on the big night; you don't want to end up serving your lady friend the gastronomic equivalent of stripes and plaids.

Red Wines

Under $10

Firesteed Pinot Noir (Oregon). Why not replace that sinking feeling with that drinking feeling? Here's a straightforward American black pinot that's as easy on the palate as it is on the wallet. Red, light, and true. Start your winin'.

La Vieille Ferme Côtes du Ventoux (Rhône, France). Enjoy a glass of liquid postcard from the beautiful hills of the southern Rhône. Goes great.

Mountain View Cabernet Sauvignon (California). Well-made, all-purpose juice from California's central coast. Contains a full day's supply of vitamin C. Don't miss Mountain View's other wines—all delicious and honest at delicious, honest prices.

Taurino Salice Salentino Riserva (Tuscany, Italy). Vintage in and vintage out, this sturdy vino rosso is a perennial favorite of valuephiles everywhere. Bottle-lickin' good.

Trapiche "Oak Cask" Malbec (Mendoza, Argentina). Oakeydokey! More than a mouthful for less than a pocketful, this woody groove juice is liquid possibility from down where the toilets flush backward. Drink globally.

Tyrell's Long Flat Red (New South Wales, Australia). No frills, but no swill either. A real workhorse and a real bargain, this is tasty, lowfalutin red hooch. Goes down so easy, it practically drinks itself.

Wyndham Estates Bin 555 Shiraz (Southeastern Australia). Que syrah syrah! Or as the Aussies say, "shiraz." This here's some hearty plonk from Down Under. Down under 10 bucks, that is!

Under $15

Argiolas Costera (Sardinia, Italy). A libation sensation from that island off the knee of Italy's boot. With gobs of soft, welcoming flavors, it's a wine with real hospitality. This red means go.

Bonny Doon Big House Red (California). A grape escape. Bonny Doon's goons blend together a hodgepodge of several disparate grape varieties, most of which rarely share a bottle. That doesn't mean you shouldn't share a bottle. This is a friendly mutt with a good personality.

Château Larose-Trintaudon Haut-Médoc (Bordeaux, France). Genuine Bordeaux rouge that you can find for a relatively modest prix fixe in nearly any olde wine shoppe. Might not knock both your socks off, but it will impair your ability to operate heavy machinery.

Clos du Bois Merlot (California). Red, willing, and able! Here's a user-friendly merlot at boozer-friendly prices. Tried and true—we've tried it, it's true.

Conde de Valdemar Crianza Rioja (Rioja, Spain). A red wine for people who think they don't like red wine. Lush, plush, and silky smooth, this Spaniard has done some time in oak barrels for a little extra flava. Guaranteed to stain the shirt of your choice.

***Cousino Macul* Cabernet Sauvignon Antiguas Riserva (Maipo Valley, Chile).** A mouth-expanding red that will put hair on your chest—and hopefully not on hers. Do yourself a big flavor: Slurp up a goblet or two of this hi-octane Bordeaux-esque hooch. You can thank us later.

***Guigal* Côtes du Rhône (Rhône, France).** Rhône wizard Guigal makes wine the old-fashioned way: He earns it. This stuff is very bad, as in good. The price-to-oomph ratio here is most appealing. Bacchus must be very pleased.

***Louis Jadot* Bourgogne Pinot Noir (Burgundy, France).** Pinot Noir is the only red grape grown in Burgundy; one swig of this and you'll understand why. This *bon ami* puts the "rouge" in "bleu, blanc, et rouge" and the "wine" in "wine and dine." And if there were a "lusty tannins" in "haute viniculture," it would put that there, too.

***Navarro Correas* Malbec (Mendoza, Argentina).** A righteous ruby-red from one of Argentina's top estates, this wine is soft and approachable, yet assertive. Kind of like your high school math teacher. When you're good and ready, this is good and red.

***Ravenswood Vintners Blend* Zinfandel (California).** And you thought zinfandels only came in white (which, confusingly, are actually pink). As faithful as your dog and more reliable than your dry cleaner, this red backs up Ravenswood's motto, "No wimpy wines." "Drink this more often," quoth the raven.

***Weinert* Merlot (Mendoza, Argentina).** A very well-endowed Argentinean. Fruit of the vine and work of human hands, this nectar of the gods truly is some spiritual drink. A little goes a long way; more goes even further. Liquid gold at liquid aluminum foil prices.

$15 and Up

***Château Lynch-Bages* Pauillac (Bordeaux, France).** A cabernet-heavy Bordeaux that is about as consistently reliable from vintage to vintage as a Bordeaux can be. (Note, however, that its price tag from vintage to vintage may not be so consistent.) As wine guru Robert M. Parker Jr. said of the 1993 offering, "The initial subdued aromas of earth, subtle red and black fruits, and oak require coaxing to unleash." Indeed.

***M. Chapoutier* Crozes-Hermitages *Les Meysonniers* (Rhône, France).** You wouldn't hit a man with glasses . . . of this. Only organically grown grapes go into this deep, dark, syrah-based beaut. Not only is it full-bodied, it's big-boned.

***Piero Antinori* Chianti Classico (Tuscany, Italy).** This swarthy Italian will make sure that your pasta bears fruit. A beefy, full-throttle bottle of classy classico. Slightly on the pricey side but worth every Euro. Up the Antinori.

***Ridge Central Coast* Zinfandel (California).** When it's time to roll out the dry red carpet, look no further. A burly brew that walks the walk and talks the talk, this potent potable is also an excellent dancer that won't step on the toes of any red meat dish.

White Wines

Under $10

Falesco **Est! Est!! Est!!! (Montefiascone, Italy).** This is a scrappy little guy—fruity and, when fresh, slightly spritzy. Knock it back with some lite chow or after you've mowed the lawn. Go Est, young man.

Joh. Jos. Prüm Riesling Kabinett (Mosel, Germany). Classic German riesling. When the nighttime is the white time, look no further than this little wienerschnitzel. We'd say it's fruity, but you might get the wrong idea. You'll wish it came in a 40-ounce bottle.

Lindemans Bin 65 Chardonnay (Southeastern Australia). Wine of the times! Fortunately, the copious accolades accorded this chard haven't inflated its head—or its price. There's a time and a place for this baby: anytime, anyplace.

S. Quirico Vernaccia di San Gimignano (Tuscany, Italy). Light, right, and outta sight. Vernaccia is reported to have been Michelangelo's favorite wine. The San Quirico is crisp and dry, a must-try.

Under $15

Beringer Founders' Estate **Chardonnay (California).** Textbook California chardonnay. Stick your schnozz in a glass of this weighty white to see what wine geeks mean by "bouquet." Rich, famous, and tailor-made for rich seafood dishes and cream sauces. Don't be a chardonnaysayer.

Casa Lapostolle Sauvignon Blanc (Rapel Valley, Chile). A Bordeaux-style sauvignon with some real ooh la la. After a bottle of this, your lady friend will be laughing with you, not at you. Drink two of these and call me in the morning.

Louis Jadot Mâcon-Villages (Burgundy, France). Betcha didn't know Burgundy produced white wines. Here's a light, bright chardonnay from one of the region's ace producers. Goes well with chicken. And things that taste like chicken.

Louis Latour Mâcon-Lugny (Burgundy, France). This rich chardonnay means business and isn't going to take *non* for an answer. Improve your French, one sip at a time. Ecoutez et répétez: "C'est delicieux!"

Pierre Sparr Gewürztraminer Carte d'Or (Alsace, France). *Gewürz* translates literally to "spice." One hit of this stuff and that will make sense. It's rich and full-bodied with a touch of well-integrated sweetness. Try and try again.

Trimbach Pinot Blanc (Alsace, France). No wonder everybody was fighting over Alsace! This smooth operator provides a refreshing alternative to chardonnay. Versatile vino for a variety of vittles.

$15 and Up

Adelsheim **Pinot Gris (Oregon).** Who says white wines can't jump? Pinot gris is Oregon's great white, and the good people at Adelsheim do it right. No pushover, this high-quality quaffable is a natural with salmon. Get grisy!

Play This

Like wine, music is an integral component of having a woman over for dinner. Music can set a mood; it can ruin a mood. It can serve as a backdrop, stimulate conversation, or fill those awkward silences. The right music can frame an unforgettable moment; the wrong music can make the entire evening a forgettable moment. The power lies in your hands.

Let's face it, no man wants to be referred to as "that guy who had me over for dinner and played *Dark Side of the Moon*." If you own a turntable or work in a record store, chances are you have a good handle on the music thing and can probably skip this section. If you're the type of guy who, when he moves, packs up the stereo last and immediately hooks it up in the new apartment, you may have stopped reading by now. However, if you own a copy of *Jock Jams* or any George Winston record, read on, my wayward son.

Your choice of music should not be distracting in content or decibels. As much as you may love AC/DC, you won't want them thrusting their balls through your speakers and onto your dinner plates. You have to admit Angus and the boys sound too loud even at the lowest of volumes.

On the flip side, while Kenny G and Yanni may be good soundtracks for shopping or getting your teeth drilled, four out of five dentists surveyed claim that a steady diet of smooth jazz or New Age can be hazardous to the health of your relationship. It's no coincidence that when you combine the words *new* and *age*, the result bears an uncanny resemblance to the word *sewage*.

So what should you play? Chances are, you're going to play whatever CDs you already have and like. But if the world of music is alien to you, or if you're simply in the market for some fresh sounds, give some of the following suggestions a spin. Here are 48 CDs that will complement your cooking even if she doesn't compliment it.

Air, *Moon Safari*. In the late '90s, Air, much like the stuff we breathe, was here, there, and everywhere: in TV commercials (Pantene shampoo), TV shows, and movie soundtracks (*The Virgin Suicides*). Electronic without the dancey beats and loungey without making you feel like a Banana Republic model, the French band's sexy and smartly swanky tunes consist of laid-back grooves speckled with bleeps and burbles that overtake your subconscious and suck you far out into the stratosphere. Millions couldn't resist the pull of the music. You won't be able to either.

Chet Baker, *The Best of Chet Baker Sings*. Chet isn't a great singer, but man, can he sing! This compilation offers up 20 of his warmest and most expressive vocal vehicles from the mid 1950s. Backed only by piano trio, Chet's swoon-inducing croon is up close and personal. And you even get a few tastes of his trumpetry. File under WAX-MELTING DREAMBOAT.

Bee Gees, *Best of Bee Gees*. Nope, "Stayin' Alive" isn't on this. Neither is "Jive Talkin'" or "You Should Be Dancing." That's because those songs stink and these songs are great. This best of contains such early Brothers Gibb ditties as "I Started a Joke," "Massachusetts," and the perennial karaoke fave "To Love Somebody."

Peter Bruntnell, *Normal for Bridgwater*. British indie-rock guy turns Americana alt-country guy—and does it very convincingly. This little-known gem, featuring members of like-minded country/rock outfit Son Volt, evokes the image of a dusty, dilapidated '70s muscle car limping off into a bursting desert sunset. Light a campfire, kick off your boots, lean back, and tune up your air guitar.

Tim Buckley, *Happy Sad*. Tim Buckley's transitional, third full-length found the Los Angeles singer-songwriter straddling the troubadour image he had previously cultivated and the more improvisational, rhythmically driven vamp-groove territory he would soon explore. Buckley's rich vocals and 12-string acoustic strumming are backed by his relaxed quartet of upright bass, vibes/marimba, congas, and lead guitar. *Happy Sad* is dominated by a loose, jazzy drift; its overriding vibe could perhaps be best described as, well, happy sad.

John Cale, *Paris 1919*. Velvet Underground co-founder and musical chameleon Cale, whose CV already included production credits on the proto-punk debuts of both The Stooges and The Modern Lovers, took a surprisingly straightforward approach with this quirky 1973 pop-rock offering. While not a concept album, per se, *Paris 1919* is woven cohesively together by a consistency of material and mood, and the singer's rich Welsh baritone. Subtle, sympathetic instrumental support is provided by members of Little Feat and tasteful orchestral flourishes lend a regal feel to these nine beautiful, predominantly low-impact, entirely infectious tunes.

Lloyd Cole, *Love Story*. Only one singer-songwriter can name-drop Simone de Beauvoir and Greta Garbo in his lyrics and still pull off writing a hell of a good song. After fronting pensive U.K. guitar-popsters Lloyd Cole and the Commotions for most of the '80s, our man moved to New York City and applied his acerbic wit to a solo career. *Love Story*, Cole's fourth solo effort, features his dark, articulate lyrics paired with simple stripped-down songs. It's an altogether lovely sounding affair. Just keep the conversation flowing so your date doesn't get bogged down in the heavy subject matter.

John Coltrane, *Lush Life*. You've got the poster, now buy the record. With his burly tenor sound, Trane tackles four standards and a blues number, sending string after string of ideas tumbling from his horn of plenty. *Lush Life*, one of his earliest leader albums, has plenty of muscular blowing but also proves that the saxophonist could interpret a ballad with delicate sensitivity. This is a snapshot of an artist poised to take the jazz world by heavy storm. Incidentally, the three trio numbers (with bass and drums) came to be only because the hired piano player missed the recording date.

Paolo Conte, *The Best of Paolo Conte*. Paolo Conte's singing career began at the ripe old age of 37. After a decade of writing hit songs for various

Italian recording artists, he released his first album in 1974 and soon became one of Italy's most revered pop icons. This 1998 collection on Elektra/Asylum consists mainly of remakes of hits from throughout his 25-year singing career. Conte's gruff and gravelly yet charming voice has the worn texture of old sandpaper. Whether he's growling, scatting, or kazooing (literally), his wild approach to vocals lets him get away with singing about everything from love to jazz to Hemingway to lemon ice cream. It's all in Italian, so don't try to figure out what he's saying. Just enjoy the ride.

Miles Davis, *Porgy and Bess*. The Pablo Picasso of jazz in his *Kind of Blue* period. Miles applies his trademark panache and understated, bulletproof, muted-trumpet sound to the entire Gershwin classic, with majestic orchestral arrangements sculpted by the forward-thinking and highly influential Gil Evans.

Nick Drake, *Pink Moon*. Sad songs say so much. This platter sees our hero out in the open, with nothing to hide behind but an acoustic guitar and a smattering of piano. Car commercial, schmar commercial: This is music that was made for the right reasons. Be advised that at just shy of a half-hour, this disc is compact. That's why your CD player is equipped with a repeat button. Believe the hype.

Francis Dunnery, *Man*. Every once in a while, there comes a record so unique that it completely changes the way you look at love, life, and what makes you happy. With *Man*, Dunnery, a singer-songwriter veteran of the music industry who's survived more ups and downs than a zipper on John Holmes's pants, delivers 12 brilliant, brutally honest songs that beg the question "Why isn't this guy more popular?" Find this disc at www.aquariannation.com.

Bob Dylan, *Nashville Skyline*. Bob goes country! But you wouldn't even know it's him from the smooth croon on this platter. (Legend has it he quit smoking several months before recording this.) Boasts the FM favorite "Lay Lady Lay" and features Johnny Cash on the unforgettable "Girl from the North Country." What your country can do for you.

Duke Ellington and His Orchestra, *. . . And His Mother Called Him Bill*. Billy Strayhorn, the composer-arranger-pianist who was the Duke's collaborator and friend of nearly 30 years, passed away in 1967. So close was their musical partnership that in the hundreds of compositions they coauthored, it was often impossible to discern which bits were written by which man. Here, the big band pay loving tribute to their friend by reprising a selection of his contributions to Ellingtonia. They play with typical urbanity and with a dignified reverence for the man who was, as the Duke himself might have said, "beyond category."

Bill Evans Trio, *Sunday at the Village Vanguard*. You've never heard a band rock so soft! One of the records that established the template for the piano trio, made by three jazz greats whose abilities as players are rivaled only by their abilities as listeners. With empathy verging on telepathy, these cats are truly playing together, not just in the same room. The Midas touch of pianist Evans, the alchemy of bassist Scott LaFaro, the textural timbres of drummer Paul Motian—this is music that's wonderful to hear and even better to listen to.

Everything but the Girl, *Amplified Heart*. Lite-jazz duo gone acoustica-pop, EBTG scored an international hit with "Missing," a tune that undoubtedly seeped into your subconscious at some point. Dominated by themes of rainy-day disillusionment, broken hearts, and long-lost romance, this disc is guaranteed to set the stage for bedroom eyes. Soft enough to allow you to carry on a conversation and serious enough to keep her from dancing.

Serge Gainsbourg, *Couleur Café*. Referred to as the dirty old man of French music, Gainsbourg was capable of charming the panties off the likes of Brigitte Bardot and Jane Birkin with his naughty lyrics, boozy persona, unfiltered cigarettes, and rotting teeth. This collection, spanning 1959 to 1975, reveals his cheeky side and delves into kitschy, hip-swinging cha-cha and mambo. Slip into your Speedo, press PLAY, and break out the martini shaker.

The Jimmy Giuffre 3, *The Jimmy Giuffre 3*. This utterly unique, drumless, pianoless trio plays, as Mr. Giuffre himself aptly called it, folk jazz. In response to what he thought had become the "tyranny of the drums" in jazz, the leader dispensed with percussion altogether and assembled this combo of bass, guitar, and his own battery of woodwinds. Here are 11 highly hummable ditties by a group with

a laid-back, big-sky, front-porch sound that's as American as hot dogs but much better for you.

Neil Halstead, *Sleeping on Roads*. You walk into a record store. A song is playing. You don't know who it is, but it has those downward-sloping melodies, those soft vocals, and that blurry-framed, sentimental, indie-rock aesthetic you have a big soft spot for. You pause to listen and instantly know that this is an album you will be leaving the store with. You walk up to the counter to ask the guy with the haircut who it is. He smiles and hands you this record.

Richard Hawley, *Late Night Final*. So Roy Orbison is dead. Or is he? In 2001, soft-spoken guitarist Hawley emerged with this astonishing solo effort. His cashmere croon and grand, canyonesque guitars will leave you wondering if he's channeling Orbison's spirit and will give you that warm, fuzzy, contented feeling—kind of like a bacon-egg-and-cheese sandwich gives you on a rainy Sunday morning.

Joe Henry, *Scar*. Very few musicians turn out quality work as consistently as Los Angeles–based songwriter Joe Henry. While *Scar* is not a concept album, this low-key rock offering follows a smooth evolution of moods, beginning on a smoky, sultry note and ending with a lonely 14-minute epic featuring the lingering, rambling wail of jazz great Ornette Coleman's alto sax. Take a listen and be glad there are a bunch of other Joe Henry CDs out there.

Billie Holiday, *Lady Day: The Best of Billie Holiday*. With a singular, less-is-more approach and plaintive, laid-back delivery, vocal stylist Billie Holiday transformed countless jazz standards into poignant personal statements. This two-disc retrospective collects the cream of her 1930s sides—arguably the finest of her career—and serves as an excellent introduction to the evocative work of a true artist.

Joe Jackson, *Night and Day*. In 1984, Jackson left behind the post-punk/ska/jumpin'-jive dalliances of his earlier records and broke into pop's mainstream with radio staples "Steppin' Out," "Breaking Us in Two," and "Real Men." Sporting a persistent urban pulse, frisky Latin beats, and Joe's signature chimelike piano, *Night and Day* evokes the romantic image of Manhattan's twinkling skyline as seen through the rain-spattered window of a late-night taxicab. Step out for this CD before she steps in for dinner.

Ronnie Lane and Slim Chance, *Anymore for Anymore*. As Ronnie Lane was putting together this record, he was on his way out of the Faces, the offshoot of the Small Faces, the band he'd cofounded 8 years before. It seems the Faces' singer, Rod Stewart, had eclipsed Ronnie, the de facto leader, in spotlight share. So in 1973, Ronnie assembled Slim Chance, a tighter band with a stronger folk and roots sensibility. On this, his first "solo" outing, acoustic guitar, mandolin, organ, saxophone, and even a little accordion underpin Ronnie's delicate vocals and lend an honest, homegrown, band-from-next-door feel. The 2003 Pilot Records reissue includes a number of tasty bonus tracks.

The Left Banke, *There's Gonna Be a Storm*. These New York popmongers combined sticky melodic hooks with delicate, lacy harmonies and bundled them up in warm orchestral settings. Dappled with period harpsichord, their 26 baroque-pop relics are '60s without sounding dated and sweet without being saccharine. The success of the band's earliest and biggest hit, "Walk Away Renée," was never duplicated, securing their status as a one-hit wonder. With all the buried treasure here, you'll wonder why they weren't a more-hits wonder.

Massive Attack, *Blue Lines*. With a bass deep enough to shake your kidneys loose and a groove smoother than Iman's legs after a waxing, *Blue Lines* is consistently hailed as a landmark album of the '90s. This is the record that earned Bristol's Massive Attack the title "grandfathers of trip-hop." A mix of trancelike beats, inspired female vocals, and whispered rapping makes this disc a must for any guy looking to spruce up a CD collection, justify buying a subwoofer, or, most important, find a beat to eat to.

Mazzy Star, *So Tonight That I Might See*. Press PLAY and let the soothing narcotic dream begin: High above the earth, a light wind blows you off a floating ledge, sending you tumbling in slow motion through miles of layered clouds. A sense of complete calm takes over as you give in to the falling feeling and glide past blinking satellites, passenger-filled planes, and migrating birds. Fifty-two minutes later, you lightly touch down on terra firma, shake your head, and wonder how soon it'll be before you ever feel this relaxed again. Includes the haunting 1993 hit "Fade into You."

Charles Mingus, *Mingus Ah Um*. Recorded in the pivotal jazz year of 1959, *Mingus Ah Um* came out of the bassist-composer-bandleader's most prolific period. Features two of his best-known compositions, the rollicking "Better Get It in Your Soul" and "Goodbye Pork Pie Hat," the classic threnody for legendary tenor tooter Lester Young, who passed away weeks before these recording sessions. The seven-piece band also tackles hat-doffing tributes to jazz pioneers Charlie Parker, Duke Ellington, and Jelly Roll Morton. From hard-rocking to solemn, and anything in between, this album covers a lot of ground but is always rooted in earthy blues and injected with plenty of church and gobs of soul.

Thelonious Monk, *Thelonious Alone in San Francisco*. Thelonious takes it to the stage tutto solo. Features some of Monk's best-known compositions and a handful of underdog standards that, once refracted by the pianist's cubist plunk, sound anything but standard. Monk lurches, lunges, and wrests as much out of the 88s as humanly possible. A better way to spend 45 minutes does not exist.

Van Morrison, *Astral Weeks*. A far cry from his now-ubiquitous "Brown-Eyed Girl" of the previous year, *Astral Weeks* was recorded with a crack team of seasoned jazz veterans in under 2 days. The result is a stunning record of loose-fitting fireside companions. A Van for all seasons.

Paul Motian, *Paul Motian on Broadway, Vols. 1–3*. An instrumental jazz group with an unmistakable sound takes a stroll down Tin Pan Alley to put their original, thoroughly modern spin on well-chosen show tunes and repertoire by Gershwin, Cole Porter, and the like. For those with rock-and-roll ears, the atmospheric guitar wizardry of Bill Frisell is a clear entrée to this music. Each of the volumes in the series is equally unpredictable and wonderful. Choose one or collect all three.

Milton Nascimento and Lô Borges, *Clube Da Esquina*. In 1972, Brazilian singer-songwriters Nascimento and Borges, along with several fellow musicians from their home state of Minas Gerais, collaborated on an album that would prove to the outside world that there was much more to Brazilian music than the samba and bossa nova. Milton's impassioned vocals slide effortlessly through the polished treatments of 21 acoustic yet lavishly arranged songs, 4 of which every Brazilian would come to know by heart. After more than 30 years, this disc still sounds remarkably fresh. With a full helping of such original, beautiful music, don't be surprised if she cries out for more in Portuguese: *"Mais! Mais!"*

Youssou N'Dour, *Guide (Wommat)*. If the occasion demands a bit of bounce in the background, reach for this vibrant Afro-pop CD. N'Dour, a Grammy-winning singer and pioneer in Senegal's music scene, rose to international fame in the mid '80s, while recording and touring with Peter Gabriel. This 1994 release contains the hit "7 Seconds," a duet with Neneh Cherry, and has our man spinning tales in French, English, and his native tongue, Wolof. Features beats that command your toes to tap and soaring vocals that make you want to fly. Everyone needs a little more N'Dour.

Willie Nelson, *Red Headed Stranger*. Having written plenty of songs that were hits for other performers, Willie was regarded throughout the '60s as more of a songwriter than a performer. But by the mid-'70s, the frequent presidential candidate's singing, songwriting, and inventive guitar playing had come entirely into their own, and his country, folk, blues, and jazz influences had crystallized into something that was entirely *his* own. *Red Headed Stranger* is a grand ole opera, a tale set in the old West that sounds like it could be the soundtrack to a Clint Eastwood film that Sergio Leone never made. Bare-bones instrumentation and direct, understated presentation paint the perfect picture. Find out why this is the record that made country music's grass-smokin'-est, tax-evadin'-est outlaw a full-blown star.

Beth Orton, *Central Reservation*. In the late '90s, Orton's sleepy, soulful voice caused the ears of the music-buying public to perk up and sent critics scrambling for the right words to praise her. With an ever-present acoustic guitar twinkling in the background, this, her second effort, finds Orton standing at the point where folk, blues, electronic, and country music intersect. Heartfelt without trying too hard, *Central Reservation* is the ideal CD when your dinner companion has her big toe in the '00s and a pinky toe in the '60s.

Joe Pass, *Virtuoso*. Eleven jazz staples and an original blues tune comprise this program of exquisitely rendered solo performances by the late guitar master. Pass plays chords and lead and bass lines simultaneously, all with a refined precision that more than justifies the title of this album. His mind-boggling technique must be heard to be believed.

The Pernice Brothers, *Overcome by Happiness*. This is a one-size-fits-all, unisex favorite from Massachusetts-based songwriter extraordinaire Joe Pernice and his associates. A dozen perfectly crafted chamber-pop pearls are nestled comfortably in lush, organic arrangements. The 12-song forecast? Partly sunny with a chance of showers.

Sam Prekop, *Sam Prekop*. Finally, a record that puts the *oo* in *smooth*! One of the main guys in Chicago's indie scene, Prekop temporarily excused himself from his band, The Sea and Cake, to record 10 luxuriously textured songs worthy of comparison to Häagen-Dazs. Prekop's airy falsetto floats atop a comfy bossa nova feel, resulting in a jazzy sophistication. The perfect soundtrack for any moment that involves cooking, eating, drinking, thinking, relaxing, or any combination of the above.

Roxy Music, *Avalon*. In 1982, seminal '70s art-rock band Roxy Music was about to call it a day when they made this sexy masterpiece. With *Avalon*, Bryan Ferry and the boys' glamorous, gold-tinged soundscapes bid adieu to their glittering past, while paving the way for the synthesizer-driven new-wave sound of the mid '80s. Make sure the fridge is stocked with eggs and OJ, because the woman you're having over for dinner might just be staying for breakfast.

Talk Talk, *Colour of Spring*. Listen listen. The one '80s band it's never too late to rediscover. The early chart success of the band's synth-pop hits "Talk Talk" and "It's My Life" overshadowed this back-to-basics record's complexity, intensity, and stripped-down instrumentation. With singer Mark Hollis's creamy vocals layered over beds of burbling organs and sparse drumbeats, you may find yourself yearning for a simpler time when hormones raged and slow dances made you walk funny.

Art Tatum, *The Art Tatum Solo Masterpieces, Vol. 4*. In 1960, Verve Records founder Norman Granz sold his label to MGM. Of the many jazz recordings that had made Verve famous—including those by Ella Fitzgerald, Billie Holiday, and Charlie Parker—Granz sold all. With the exception, that is, of those made by piano giant Art Tatum. Here's a cluster of Tatum's finest piano solos culled from the mountain of material he recorded for Verve in the mid '50s. Of the blind maestro's many recordings, these particularly showcase his astonishing virtuosity, harmonic sophistication, and digital dexterity. Earth-shattering pianistics, groundbreaking jazz, exciting listening.

Various Artists, *Brazil Classics 1: Beleza Tropical*. Compiled by Brazilophile and former head Talking Head David Byrne, this collection draws on the deep well of infectious Brazilian pop music of the 1970s and early '80s. Sing along in phonetic Portuguese.

Sarah Vaughan, *After Hours*. Jazz diva "Sassy" breaks it down with just guitar and bass backing and comes out swinging, albeit lightly. Sarah makes the most of the intimate setting as she fans the flames on a set of slow-burn ballads. Break out the bearskin rug, toss the wine glasses into the fireplace, and get Sassy!

The Velvet Underground, *Loaded*. In response to an Atlantic Records exec's request for an album "loaded with hits," Lou "Mr. New York" Reed banged out 10 surprisingly accessible, mostly up-beat pop-rockers of clever simplicity, including the radio-friendly "Sweet Jane." Rhino Records's expanded *Fully Loaded* edition appends a number of contemporaneous outtakes and demos that weren't issued on the original release, all of which are equally superb. Simply great rock and roll.

Tom Waits, *Closing Time*. Waits's first long player and possibly his best. Twelve songs of urban loneliness and late-night barroom brooding, played on acoustic instruments and sweetened with the occasional strings. Recorded before the booze, smokes, and diner coffee turned his voice into a gruff bark, this record announced a fresh, post-beatnik, jazz-informed singer-songwriter-raconteur—hep cat—and a true original. Jazzy, but not jazz.

Paul Weller, *Paul Weller*. After 15 years leading both late-'70s mod trio The Jam and mid-'80s jazz-popsters The Style Council, Paul Weller opted to go solo with this 1992 "comeback debut." Showcasing a grown-up, mellower Weller, this disc reveals a rock icon who's confident dabbling in smooth soul and acid jazz beats. A tight group of tunes that will have your goldfish shimmying with your fern and will make you wish you were more comfortable with the whole dancing thing.

Zero 7, *Simple Things*. Having spent most of the '90s behind the scenes in London recording studios serving tea to rock's glitterati, studio assistants–turned-engineers Henry Binns and Sam Hardaker emerged in 1999 as production masterminds of Zero 7, a half-instrumental, half-vocal, soul-pop music collective. Often called the "British Air" (see our very first review) for their similar laid-back atmospheric grooves, Zero 7 subtracts Air's lounge feel and adds a pinch of R & B and funk, making for an immaculately produced slice of CD.

The Zombies, *Odyssey & Oracle*. Don't let the psychedelic cover art fool you. Sure it's 1968, but there are no flaming guitars, backward tapes, or studio trickery here—just glorious harmonies and melody-driven pop from the fab five. The anthemic "Time of the Season" is in there, but that's just the tip of the iceberg. Pick Big Beat Records's 1998 reissue of this classic for a whole mess of equally splendiferous extra tunes.

Red Meat

What It Really Is:
Steak, Potatoes, Green Beans, and Salad

What You Tell Her It Is:
New York Strip Steak in a Cracked Black Pepper & Whole Grain Mustard Marinade, with Roasted Red Potatoes, Sautéed String Beans, & Salad of Belgian Endive, Apples, Walnuts, & Blue Cheese

Cooking time, from prep to plate:
approximately 90 minutes

Carnophile

Is it possible for a meal to be both square and well-rounded? Funny you should ask. With all four food groups accounted for, this anti-tofu carnophile banquet boasts beef that would make Jabba the Hutt grunt and any Catholic schoolgirl blush giddily. Grab a tankard of mead, hold on to your aorta, and prepare to eat like a Viking.

Ingredients to Buy

2	shallots
1	jar whole grain mustard
2	boneless New York strip steaks (¾ pound each)
2	heads Belgian endive
1	Granny Smith apple
¼	pound shelled walnuts
¼	pound blue cheese
1	bunch fresh Italian (flat-leaf) parsley
10-12	medium red potatoes
2	large handfuls green beans

SHOPPING TIP: New York strip steaks are also called shell steaks. (We're not sure what makes them "New York" steaks. Just be thankful they're not New Jersey strip steaks.)

SHOPPING TIP: Shaped like a small, unshucked ear of corn, Belgian endive has white, yellow-tipped leaves.

Red potatoes fell out of favor back in the days of McCarthyism. Now these pinkos are back and redder than ever. You can't keep a good tuber down.

Ingredients You Should Already Have

2 cloves garlic
1 bottle balsamic vinegar
1 box kosher salt
2 tablespoons fresh ground + millful black peppercorns
1 bottle extra virgin olive oil
½ stick salted butter

If you're aroused by the idea of extra virgin olive oil, you're a sick man.

Kitchen Equipment

Cutting board Chef's and/or paring knives 2 mixing bowls Whisk 2 small plates Plastic wrap
Large baking pan Timer Aluminum foil Medium saucepan Strainer Small baking pan
Large frying pan Meat thermometer 2 dinner plates

Hold a steak up to a map of the world. Which country does it most resemble? Consider not only its outline but also its fat striations and their resemblance to bodies of water and/or land formations.

Wonder what Granny Smith did to get an apple named after her. (Maybe she was just a sour tart.)

DID YOU KNOW? The mold in blue cheese contains penicillin, despite the fact that this cheese is available over the counter.

1 Set the oven to 400°F.

2 Make the marinade for the steak: Cut the tops off the shallots, then peel off and discard the skins. Slice 1 shallot into thin, round slices and set them aside. Dice the other shallot and put it in one of the mixing bowls. Peel the garlic and discard the paper husks. Finely dice the garlic and add it to the bowl. Add ½ cup whole grain mustard and ½ cup balsamic vinegar. Add 1 tablespoon salt. Grind in about 2 tablespoons pepper. Mix. Whisk in 2 tablespoons oil. Add the steaks to the marinade and flip them to coat evenly. Put the bowl in the fridge.

3 Make the salad: Cut off the butt ends of the endive heads. Peel off and discard the outermost endive leaves. Separate what's left of the heads into individual leaves. On the small plates, arrange the leaves in sunflower formation, rounded side down. Rinse the apple, cut out and discard the core, and dice the rest into ¼" cubes. Fill each endive leaf with apple chunks. Grab a handful of walnuts, crush it in your fist, and scatter the pieces over the salads. With your fingers, crumble the blue cheese evenly over both plates. Lightly drizzle oil over the salads. Cover the salads with plastic wrap and put them in the fridge.

4 Make the potatoes: Rinse a handful of parsley and shake it dry. Cut off and discard the stems. Finely chop the leaves. Rinse the potatoes, cut them into quarters, and place them in the other mixing bowl. Add ¼ cup oil and ¼ cup chopped parsley. Salt and pepper lightly, then toss. Put the potatoes in the large baking pan. Place the pan on the middle oven rack. Set the timer to 20 minutes.

In progress: Steaks soaking, salad chilling, potatoes baking
Time remaining: 60 minutes
Things left to do: Boil and sauté beans, broil steaks

Get
Cooking

1 When the timer goes off, give the potatoes a quick stir. Then reset the timer for another 15 minutes, and when it goes off again, check the spuds. If they're golden brown and tender when you stab them with a knife, they're done. Remove them from the oven, cover the pan with foil, and place it on the stovetop to keep it warm.

2 Turn on your broiler. Pull the steaks out of the fridge to let them come to room temperature.

3 Start the beans: Fill the medium saucepan half full of water and put it on the stove over medium-high heat. Put the green beans in the strainer and rinse. Cut off and discard the stems. When the pan of water starts to boil, add the beans and cook until they're bright green (1½ to 2 minutes). Turn off the burner, pour the beans into the strainer to drain, and rinse them under cold water. Set them aside.

4 Cook the steaks: Place them in the small baking pan, and discard the marinade that's left behind in the bowl. Put the baking pan in the broiler or, if your broiler is in your oven, put the pan in there, on the top rack. The steaks will take only 5 to 8 minutes. Ask your lady friend how she likes hers done. Continue with step 5, but keep an eye on the meat.

5 It's time to finish the beans: Melt the butter in the large frying pan over medium-high heat. Add the sliced shallot and cook until soft. Add the beans and cook for 2 to 3 minutes, stirring frequently. Remove the pan from the heat, turn off the burner, and lightly salt and pepper the beans.

6 Check on the steaks. For medium-rare, cook them for 5 to 6 minutes (flip after 3 minutes), or until the meat thermometer registers 145°F when stuck in the center of the steaks; for medium, cook for 7 to 8 minutes (flip after 4 minutes), or to 160°F. When they're done, turn off the broiler and pull out the pan.

7 Arrange the steaks on the dinner plates with the potatoes and the beans so everything looks tasty. Remove the salads from the fridge and serve.

Your sacrifice has been duly noted. Rufus the Meat God is pleased with you.

Drink This

Mountain View Cabernet Sauvignon, <$10

Château Larose-Trintaudon Haut-Médoc, <$15

Clos du Bois Merlot, <$15

Play This

Serge Gainsbourg, *Couleur Café*

Billie Holiday, *Lady Day: The Best of Billie Holiday*

Sam Prekop, *Sam Prekop*

What It Really Is:

Steak and Potatoes with Spinach and Shrimp

What You Tell Her It Is:

Garlic-&-Herb–Marinated Filet Mignon with Horseradish Cream Sauce, Served with Baked Potatoes, Sautéed Spinach, & Shrimp Cocktail

Cooking time, from prep to plate:
approximately 90 minutes

Tag Team

The answer to those age-old questions "Where's the beef?" and "Where's the crustacean?," this surf-and-turf tag team will put meat on her bones and lead in your pencil. Start sharpening those eyeteeth; this is a meat-tacular carnevale any way you slice it. Not for practicing Hindus.

Ingredients to Buy

2	baking potatoes
1	bunch fresh Italian (flat-leaf) parsley
1	bottle Worcestershire sauce
2	filet mignon steaks (½ pound each)
1	container (16 ounces) sour cream
1	bottle prepared horseradish sauce
1	bunch fresh chives
8-12	colossal shrimp, cooked and peeled
1	lemon
1	bottle cocktail sauce
2	bags prewashed baby spinach

Before Mentos, there was parsley, the original fresh maker.

Ingredients You Should Already Have

4 cloves garlic
1 jar Dijon mustard
1 bottle extra virgin olive oil
1 box kosher salt
Millful black peppercorns
1 bottle finely ground white pepper
1 stick salted butter

DID YOU KNOW? One of the primary goals of European exploration in the 1400s was to find a more direct trade route to the peppercorn-producing Far East.

Kitchen Equipment

Cutting board   Chef's and/or paring knives   2 mixing bowls   Whisk   Plastic wrap   2 cereal bowls
3 small plates   Aluminum foil   Small baking pan   Meat thermometer   Large frying pan
2 dinner plates

1 Set the oven to 400°F.

2 Scrub the potatoes under running water. Use a fork to poke four sets of holes in each.

3 Give the potatoes a head start: Place them on the middle oven rack. They'll need to bake for 45 to 60 minutes. Note the time and take the next 15 minutes to work on your moonwalk before moving on to step 4.

4 Make the marinade for the steak: Peel the garlic and discard the paper husks. Finely dice the garlic and put it in one of the mixing bowls. Rinse a handful of parsley and shake it dry. Cut off and discard the stems. Finely chop the leaves. Add them to the bowl. Add ½ cup Worcestershire sauce and 4 tablespoons mustard. Whisk. Whisk in ¼ cup oil. Lightly salt and grind in black pepper. Add the steaks and flip them to coat evenly. Put the bowl in the fridge.

5 In the other mixing bowl, combine half of the sour cream, 2 tablespoons horse-radish, 1 teaspoon salt, and 1 teaspoon white pepper. Cover the bowl with plastic wrap and put it in the fridge. This is the sauce for your filet mignon. Incidentally, filet mignon literally means "dainty filet." (We don't get it either.)

6 Whisk the remaining sour cream until it's smooth and place it in a cereal bowl. Finely chop the chives and whisk them into the sour cream. Cover the bowl with plastic wrap and put it in the fridge. Unwrap the butter while it is cold (unwrapping warm butter is like trying to peel a rotten banana), place it on a small plate, and put the plate on the table. The butter and sour cream will be the potato toppings.

7 Once the potatoes have been in the oven for 30 minutes, flip them.

Wait 15 minutes before continuing with "Get Cooking" step 1.

In progress: Potatoes baking, steaks soaking, sauces chilling
Time remaining: 20 to 30 minutes
Things left to do: Make shrimp cocktail, broil steaks, sauté spinach

Get
Cooking

1 Turn on your broiler. Pull the steaks out of the fridge to let them come to room temperature.

2 By now, the potatoes should be done. Stab one with a knife to double-check; when it's soft all the way through, the spuds are ready. Remove them from the oven, wrap them with foil, and place them on the stovetop to keep warm.

3 Make the shrimp cocktail: Get ready to do some garnishing with sprigs. This is a real résumé builder. On each of 2 small plates, arrange an even number of shrimp in a radial fan formation. Slice the lemon into wedges and place 2 wedges on each plate. Garnish each plate with a couple sprigs of parsley. Pour the cocktail sauce into a cereal bowl and put it in the fridge, along with the shrimp.

4 Cook the steaks: Place them in the small baking pan, and put the pan in the broiler or, if your broiler is in your oven, put the pan in there, on the top rack. The steaks will take only 6 to 8 minutes, so keep an eye on them. Ask your lady friend how she likes hers done. For medium-rare, cook them for 5 to 6 minutes (flip them after 3 minutes), or until the thermometer registers 145°F when stuck in the center of the steaks; for medium, cook for 7 to 8 minutes (flip after 4 minutes), or to 160°F.

5 Make the spinach: Pour 2 tablespoons oil into the large frying pan and put it on the stove over medium heat. When the oil is hot (when it looks runny), add spinach a handful at a time. Cook for 2 to 3 minutes, until wilted. Lightly salt and pepper. Cover the pan, remove it from the heat, and turn off the burner.

6 Check on the steaks: If they're done, turn off the broiler and pull out the pan.

7 Arrange the filets, potatoes, and spinach on the dinner plates so they look appetizing. Double-check that all of the burners are turned off. Take the horseradish cream out of the fridge and put a small dollop on top of each steak. Garnish the cream with a sprig of parsley. Put the remaining horseradish sauce and chivey sour cream on the table.

Listen, there's a steak calling your name. (Actually, if this is true, you haven't cooked it enough.)

Shrimp cocktail is done. If your guest has arrived, feel free to dig in, as the rest of the meal won't take long to prepare.

Drink This

Trapiche "Oak Cask" Malbec, <$10

Weinert Merlot, <$15

Château Lynch-Bages Pauillac, $15+

Play This

Bill Evans Trio, *Sunday at the Village Vanguard*

Mazzy Star, *So Tonight That I Might See*

Sarah Vaughan, *After Hours*

What It Really Is:
Beef-Asparagus Stir-Fry with Rice and Soybeans

What You Tell Her It Is:
Orange-Ginger Sticky Beef Stir-Fry with Asparagus Served over a Bed of Sticky Rice, with Edamame

Cooking time, from prep to plate:
approximately 90 minutes

Sticky

Learn Japan-ease in a little over an hour: This fruit, root, and shoot triumvirate is far from tricky and even further from icky. It's an extravaganza of semisweet stick-to-itiveness, the taste sensation that spawned the recent dance craze The Sticky Beef—and the X-rated film of the same name.

Ingredients to Buy

1	4" piece fresh ginger
1	small box dark brown sugar
1	small container fresh orange juice
1	bottle rice wine vinegar
1¼	pounds beef filet
1	bunch asparagus
1	bag sushi rice
1	bunch scallions
1	bag (1 pound) frozen edamame
2	handfuls bean sprouts
8	ounces toasted sesame seeds

Edamame (green soybeans) are regularly accorded mad props by Japanese hip-hop artists.

DID YOU KNOW? Ripe sesame pods will burst open when touched. Which explains the origin of the phrase OPEN SESAME, the words Ali Baba used to gain entry to the robbers' cave in the story of Ali Baba and the 40 Thieves.

Ingredients You Should Already Have

4 cloves garlic
1 bottle soy sauce
1 bottle toasted sesame oil
1 box kosher salt

Soy sauce comes in both regular and low-sodium varieties. Choose the one you want depending on how much water you'd like you and your lady friend to retain.

Kitchen Equipment

Chef's and/or paring knives   Cutting board   Mixing bowl   Whisk   Strainer
Small saucepan with lid   Timer   Medium saucepan   Salad bowl   Cereal bowl
2 large frying pans   2 dinner plates

1 If you will be drinking white wine, put it in the fridge. Use the paring knife to remove the skin from the ginger. Discard the skin. Finely chop about 3 tablespoons of ginger and set it aside.

2 Make the marinade for the beef: This is where things start to get sticky. Ready the Handi Wipes. Peel 2 of the garlic cloves and discard the paper husks. Finely dice the garlic and put it in the mixing bowl. Add 2 tablespoons of the chopped ginger, $1\frac{1}{2}$ cups brown sugar, $\frac{1}{2}$ cup soy sauce, $\frac{1}{2}$ cup orange juice, and $\frac{1}{4}$ cup vinegar. Mix thoroughly. Whisk in $\frac{1}{4}$ cup sesame oil. Set aside.

3 Cut the filet into $\frac{1}{4}$"-thick slices and submerge them in the marinade. Put the bowl in the fridge. The beef will need to soak for at least 1 hour. Note the time and continue with steps 4 through 6.

Advisory: Eating asparagus makes your pee smell funkier than James Brown's pants after a marathon show.

4 Rinse the asparagus, then cut off and discard the butts (the bottom 1" to 2"; asparagus butts can be tougher than Mr. T's toenails, so do yourself a favor and lop those babies off). Cut each spear diagonally into three sections. Set aside. Dice the remaining 2 garlic cloves and set aside.

5 Pour $1\frac{1}{4}$ cups rice into the strainer. (Some famous chefs have their own personal strainer.) Swish the rice around under cold running water until the water runs clear. Shake off the excess water and set aside.

6 Rinse the scallions and shake dry. Cut off and discard the roots. Starting from the root end, cut the bottom 5" of each scallion into thin, round slices. Set aside.

When the beef has soaked for an hour, continue with "Get Cooking" step 1.

In progress: Wine chilling, beef soaking
Time remaining: 20 to 25 minutes
Things left to do: Cook rice, boil edamame, stir-fry asparagus, stir-fry beef

Get Cooking

1. Cook the rice: Pour 1¼ cups water into the small saucepan. Add the rinsed rice and a pinch of salt. Cover the pan and place it on the stove over medium-high heat. When the water starts to boil, turn down the heat to the lowest setting. Simmer for 15 minutes. Continue with step 2 but don't forget about the rice—set the timer to 15 minutes. When the timer goes off, turn off the heat but leave the pan covered.

2. Make the edamame: Fill the medium saucepan half full of water. Add a pinch of salt. Put the pan on the stove over medium-high heat. When the water starts to boil, add the edamame. Cook for 3 to 5 minutes, until they float. When they're done, pour into the strainer to drain. Dump them into the salad bowl, salt lightly, and serve now (hot) or with dinner (cooler). Set the cereal bowl on the table to hold the empty pods.

3. Pour 2 tablespoons sesame oil into a large frying pan and put it on the stove over medium-high heat. When the oil is hot (when it looks runny), add the remaining chopped garlic and the remaining 1 tablespoon of chopped ginger. Cook, stirring, for 1 minute (be careful not to burn the garlic). Add the asparagus and cook until bright green (about 3 minutes). Add the bean sprouts and 4 splashes soy sauce. Give it a quick stir and remove it from the heat.

4. Get started cooking the beef: Pour 2 tablespoons sesame oil into the other large frying pan and put it on the stove over high heat. When the oil is hot, add the beef and cook until the pieces are brown on both sides (about 1½ minutes per side). You may have to cook the beef in 2 batches.

5. While the beef is cooking, mound half of the rice in the center of each plate. Spoon the asparagus around the rice. When the beef is done, place it on top of the asparagus. Spoon on extra juice. Sprinkle with the sliced scallions and the sesame seeds. Turn off any burners.

You just sowed some serious seeds. Reap what you have sown.

How to eat edamame:
Squeeze the beans out of a pod with your teeth but do not eat the pod. Chew, swallow, and repeat.

Drink This

Joh. Jos. Prüm Riesling Kabinett, <$10

Ravenswood Vintners Blend Zinfandel, <$15

Argiolas Costera, <$15

Play This

Joe Jackson, *Night and Day*

Art Tatum, *Art Tatum Solo Masterpieces, Vol. 4*

Zero 7, *Simple Things*

What It Really Is:
Veal with Pasta and Asparagus

What You Tell Her It Is:
Veal Saltimbocca over Linguine, with Chilled Asparagus Salad

Cooking time, from prep to plate:
75 to 90 minutes

Italicized

Seal the deal and make her squeal with this real veal meal. High-ranking representatives from the fauna and flora kingdoms join forces to yield some red, white, and green Italicized mobster chow that is nothing short of scrumpdillyicious. It's the veal of dreams: If you cook it, she'll come over.

Ingredients to Buy

1	bunch asparagus
1	Roma (plum) tomato
1	container (8 ounces) freshly grated Parmesan cheese
1	bunch fresh sage
2	ounces prosciutto, sliced paper-thin
1	shallot
1	bunch fresh Italian (flat-leaf) parsley
1	small bag all-purpose flour
1	pound veal cutlets (veal scallops)
1	box linguine
1	half bottle (375 milliliters) white wine
1	can (14½ ounces) chicken broth

DID YOU KNOW? The Italian word *saltimbocca* translates exactly to "jump in the mouth."

SHOPPING TIP: Look for freshly grated Parmesan in the refrigerated cheese section of the grocery store. Do not settle for the nonrefrigerated, faux-cheese alternative in the green can.

Sage recently did a reunion tour with Parsley, Rosemary, and Thyme.

SHOPPING TIP: Prosciutto is aged, dry-cured Italian ham. Aged, in this case, is a good thing.

Ingredients You Should Already Have

1 bottle extra virgin olive oil
1 bottle balsamic vinegar
1 box kosher salt
2 teaspoons fresh ground + millful black peppercorns
1 stick salted butter

Kitchen Equipment

Medium saucepan   Cutting board   Chef's and/or paring knives   Strainer   2 mixing bowls
3 dinner plates   Plastic wrap   Stockpot   Small plate   Large frying pan   Small baking pan
Aluminum foil   Whisk

1 If you will be drinking white wine, put it in the fridge.

2 Make the asparagus salad: Fill the medium saucepan half full of water and put it on the stove over medium-high heat. Rinse the asparagus, then cut off and discard the butts (the bottom 1" to 2"). Rinse the tomato and cut it in half. Scoop out the seeds and discard. Finely dice the tomato and set it aside. When the water starts to boil, add the asparagus and cook until bright green (about 3 minutes). Pour into the strainer to drain and rinse under cold water. Turn off the burner. Put the asparagus in a mixing bowl and lightly drizzle it with the oil and vinegar. Toss. Arrange the asparagus spears in a pinwheel formation on a dinner plate. Top with the diced tomato. Sprinkle with 1 tablespoon Parmesan. Lightly salt and grind on pepper. Cover the plate with plastic wrap and put it in the fridge.

3 Stack 8 sage leaves and roll lengthwise (like you would roll a, um, cigarette). Cut crosswise into thin slices. Repeat until you have ¼ cup sliced sage. Set aside. Repeat the process with all of the prosciutto.

4 Cut the top off the shallot. Peel off and discard the skin. Finely dice, then set aside. Rinse a handful of parsley and shake it dry. Cut off and discard the stems. Finely chop the leaves and set aside.

5 Fill the stockpot half full of water and put it on the stove over high heat. Add 1 tablespoon oil and 1 teaspoon salt. This will be for the linguine.

6 In the other mixing bowl, combine ½ cup flour, 2 teaspoons salt, and 2 teaspoons fresh ground pepper. Mix thoroughly and set aside.

7 Put the butter on the small plate and slice it into eight 1-tablespoon squares (tablespoon measurements are indicated on the butter wrapper). Put it in the fridge.

In progress: Wine chilling, salad chilling
Things left to do: Fry veal, boil linguine, make sauce
Time remaining: 30 to 45 minutes

Get
Cooking

1 Set the oven to 200°F.

2 Get started cooking the veal: Put 1 square of butter and 1 tablespoon oil in the large frying pan and put it on the stove over medium-high heat. Place 1 veal cutlet at a time in the flour mixture and flip to coat both sides evenly. When the butter is melted, add the cutlets and cook until golden brown (2 to 3 minutes per side). You may have to cook the cutlets in 2 batches. Put the veal in the small baking pan. Cover the pan with foil and put it in the oven to keep warm.

3 By now, the water for the linguine should be boiling. Reduce the heat to medium-high and cook 2 servings' worth, following the directions on the pasta box.

4 Make the sauce: Add 1 square of butter to the frying pan (the same one you used for the veal) and keep it over medium-high heat. When the butter is melted, add the diced shallot and cook until soft. Add ½ cup wine and stir it around to loosen the crispy breading remnants. Cook until the liquid has almost evaporated. Add 1 cup broth, the chopped sage, and the chopped prosciutto. Bring to a boil. Cook until half of the liquid has evaporated; this will take 5 to 8 minutes. Turn off the burner and whisk in 5 squares of butter, 1 square at a time. Salt and grind in pepper to taste.

5 When the linguine is done, pour into the strainer to drain and shake off the excess water. Turn off the burner and put the linguine back in the pot. Salt and pepper lightly. Add ½ cup Parmesan, 2 tablespoons oil, and the remaining square of butter. Toss.

6 Divide the pasta between 2 dinner plates. Place an equal number of veal cutlets on top of each pasta mound. Turn off the oven. Spoon the sauce over the veal and lightly sprinkle with the chopped parsley. Remove the salad from the fridge and serve.

We love your moxie, baby. Now eat up.

Drink This

Beringer Founders' Estate
Chardonnay, <$15

Louis Jadot
Mâcon-Villages, <$15

M. Chapoutier
Crozes-Hermitages
Les Meysonniers, $15+

Play This

Paolo Conte, *The Best of Paolo Conte*

Nick Drake, *Pink Moon*

Beth Orton,
Central Reservation

What It Really Is:
Lamb Chops, Veggies, and Salad

What You Tell Her It Is:
Pan-Seared, Rosemary-Infused Lamb Rib Chops with Oven-Roasted Yams, Blanched Sugar Snap Peas, & Mesclun Salad with Feta Cheese

Cooking time, from prep to plate:
approximately 90 minutes

Rock Star

To die for! But don't do anything rash. Show her you're the alpha male with this beta carotene–protein, lamb-yam spectacular. The rosemary-lamb combo throws a drool-inducing aroma that will have any carnivorous female treating you like a rock star. And you don't even have to wear leather pants.

Ingredients to Buy

2	yams
1	package fresh rosemary
6	lamb rib chops ($\frac{1}{4}$ pound each)
3	handfuls sugar snap peas
1	bag prewashed mesclun salad mix
1	container (12 ounces) crumbled feta cheese

Yams look like large, orange potatoes. Pick the two that look the least like Gérard Depardieu's nose.

SHOPPING TIP: Mesclun is just a fancy word for a mix of non-hallucinogenic salad greens. You may also see it sold as mixed baby greens.

Ingredients You Should Already Have

1 bottle extra virgin olive oil
1 box kosher salt
Millful black peppercorns
1 stick salted butter
1 bottle balsamic vinegar

DID YOU KNOW? Peppercorns were once so highly valued that they were used as currency.

Kitchen Equipment

Baking sheet   Cutting board   Chef's and/or paring knives   3 dinner plates   Plastic wrap
Salad bowl   Cereal bowl   Medium saucepan with lid   Large frying pan   Aluminum foil
Large baking pan   Strainer   2 small plates   Meat thermometer

1 Set the oven to 400°F.

2 Employees must wash yams before cooking: Scrub the yams under running water. Use a fork to poke four sets of holes in each.

3 Give the yams a head start—undercooked yam tastes like shoe. Put them on the baking sheet and slide the sheet onto the middle oven rack. Take the next half hour to clean your place and trim your nose hair. After 30 minutes, flip the yams and move on to step 4.

4 Remove the needles from 4 sprigs of the rosemary. Discard the stems and chop the needles as finely as possible.

5 Place the lamb chops on a dinner plate. Drizzle with ¼ cup oil. Sprinkle each with rosemary so both sides have pieces stuck to them. Lightly salt and grind on pepper. Cover the plate with plastic wrap and put it in the fridge.

6 Grab the stem of each pea pod and peel the string off the top. Discard all the strings. Set aside the pods.

7 Get started on the salad: Open the bag of mesclun and dump the greens into the salad bowl. Add the feta. Cover the salad with plastic wrap and put it in the fridge.

8 Unwrap the butter, put it on a small plate, and put it on the table. This will be for the yams.

In progress: Yams baking, lamb soaking, salad chilling
Time remaining: 20 to 30 minutes
Things left to do: Brown and broil lamb, boil peas, dress salad

Who is Emeril Lagasse's favorite TV personality?

(a) Emeril

(b) Emeril

(c) Emeril

(d) All of the above

Get Cooking

1. Fill the medium saucepan half full of water. Cover and put the pan on the stove over medium heat. This will be for the peas. Pull the lamb out of the fridge to let it come to room temperature.

2. Get started cooking the lamb: Pour 1 tablespoon oil into the large frying pan and put it on the stove over medium-high heat. When the oil is hot (when it looks runny), add the lamb and cook for 30 seconds to 1 minute on each side, until brown.

3. After the yams have cooked for an hour, remove them from the oven, wrap them with foil, and place them on the stovetop to keep warm. Turn on your broiler.

4. Continue cooking the lamb: Grease the large baking pan with a little oil and put in the chops. When the broiler has heated up, put the pan in there or, if your broiler is in your oven, put the pan in there, on the top rack. Broil for 5 to 7 minutes, keeping an eye on the chops.

5. By now, the saucepan of water should be boiling. Add the peas and cook for 1 minute. Pour the peas into the strainer to drain, and turn off the burner. Put the peas back in the saucepan, drizzle them with a little oil, and salt and grind on pepper to taste. Cover to keep warm.

6. Dress the salad: Drizzle it with oil and vinegar. Lightly salt and grind on pepper. Toss. Place it on the table with 2 small plates for serving.

7. Check on the lamb: Insert the thermometer into a chop to see whether it's cooked to your liking. It should register 145°F for medium-rare, 160°F for medium, or 165°F for well-done. When it's done, turn off the broiler and remove the chops.

8. Arrange the lamb, peas, and yams on 2 dinner plates so they look good.

Dinner is served. You just cooked a serious meal. Act like you do it every day.

Drink This

Wyndham Estates Bin 555
Shiraz, <$10

Ridge Central Coast
Zinfandel, $15+

M. Chapoutier
Crozes-Hermitages
Les Meysonniers, $15+

Play This

John Coltrane, *Lush Life*

Joe Henry, *Scar*

Van Morrison, *Astral Weeks*

What It Really Is:
Steak Tacos, Black Beans, and Chips with Salsa

What You Tell Her It Is:
Marinated Skirt Steak Tacos with Sautéed Black Beans, Red Peppers, & Corn, Served with Fresh Salsa & Guacamole

**Cooking time, from prep to plate:
approximately 90 minutes,
plus overnight marinating**

Swagger

Give your lady friend the finger food! This big-'n'-boozy beef-'n'-bean bonanza comes equipped with a zippy, south-of-the-border twang and more bite and swagger than a rabid hound. It's a relaxed, low-brow Cal-Mex smorgasbord of quality and quantity. Have your steak and eat it, too.

Ingredients to Buy

2	bunches fresh cilantro
1	bottle or can (12 ounces) beer
1	bottle Patrón tequila
1½	pounds skirt steak
2	small red onions
2	ears fresh or 1 small bag frozen corn
1	red bell pepper
4	Roma (plum) tomatoes
1	lemon
2	limes
2	avocados
1	can (14 ounces) black beans, drained
1	package (12) 6" flour tortillas
1	bag corn tortilla chips

DID YOU KNOW? Tequila is distilled from the agave, a plant that must grow for at least 7 years before it is harvested. In order to be labeled TEQUILA, the drink must be produced in or around the town of Tequila, Mexico.

Pick onions that look like they're having self-esteem problems.

SHOPPING TIP: Avocados are ripe when they are slightly soft to the touch. Ripe avocados also generally have darker skin.

Ingredients You Should Already Have

6 cloves garlic

1 bottle soy sauce

1 bottle extra virgin olive oil

1 box kosher salt

Millful black peppercorns

Kitchen Equipment

Cutting board   Chef's and/or paring knives   4 mixing bowls   Whisk   Plastic wrap   Strainer
Large frying pan with lid   Aluminum foil   Salad bowl   Small baking pan or a grill
Meat thermometer   3 dinner plates

1 Pull out one of the tortillas and wear it as a yarmulke.

2 Make the marinade for the steak: Rinse 1 bunch of the cilantro and shake it dry. Cut off and discard the stems. Finely chop the leaves and put them in a mixing bowl. Peel 5 of the garlic cloves and discard the paper husks. Finely dice and add to the mixing bowl. Add the beer, 1 cup soy sauce, and ¼ cup tequila. Stir. Whisk in ½ cup oil. Add the steak and flip it to coat evenly. Cover the bowl with plastic wrap and put it in the fridge. The steak will need to soak for at least 1 hour or, preferably, overnight for optimal tenderness. Note the time and continue with steps 3 through 5.

Little-known factoid: Most herb-chopping injuries occur within 1 mile of home.

3 Cut off the onion tops. Peel off and discard the skins. Finely dice the onions and set them aside. Rinse the remaining bunch of cilantro and shake dry. Cut off and discard the stems. Finely chop the leaves and set aside. If the corn is fresh, shuck it, then cut the kernels off the cobs and set them aside. Peel the remaining garlic clove and discard the paper husk. Finely chop the garlic and set aside. Cut the bell pepper in half. Remove and discard the stem and seeds. Dice the bell pepper into small squares and set aside.

4 Make the salsa: Rinse the tomatoes and cut them in half. Scoop out the seeds and discard. Dice the tomatoes and put them in a second mixing bowl. Add ¼ cup of the diced onion and ¼ cup of the diced cilantro. Cut the lemon and 1 of the limes in half. Set the strainer in the bowl. Hold half of the lemon and half of the lime above the strainer and squeeze the juice out of them. Discard the squeezed rinds, seeds, and pulp, and set aside the remaining lemon and lime halves. Remove the strainer from the bowl. Lightly salt the salsa and mix thoroughly. Taste to make sure it is salted to your liking. Cover the bowl with plastic wrap and put it in the fridge.

5 Make the guacamole: Cut the avocados into quarters (like you would cut pears). Remove the pits and peel off the skins, discarding both. Put the avocados into a third mixing bowl and mash them with a fork until chunky/creamy. Add ¼ cup of the diced onion and ¼ cup of the chopped cilantro. Set the strainer in the bowl. Hold the remaining lemon and lime halves above the strainer and squeeze the juice out of them. Discard the rinds, seeds, and pulp. Remove the strainer from the bowl and scrape off any guac that stuck to it. Lightly salt and grind pepper onto the guac. Mix thoroughly. Taste to make sure it is seasoned to your liking. Cut the remaining whole lime into round slices and place them on top of the guac to keep it from turning brown. Cover the bowl with plastic wrap and put it in the fridge.

Assuming the steak has soaked for an hour or overnight, continue with "Get Cooking" step 1.

In progress: Steak soaking, salsa chilling, guacamole chilling
Time remaining: 20 to 30 minutes
Things left to do: Cook steak, cook beans, warm tortillas

Besides improving guac, limes can also be an effective agent in masking the taste of crappy Mexican beer.

Get
Cooking

If your guest has arrived, dig in to the chips and dips.

Drink This

Tyrell's **Long Flat Red,** <$10

Cousino Macul **Cabernet Sauvignon Antiguas Riserva,** <$15

Beer of your choice

Play This

Chet Baker,
The Best of Chet Baker Sings

Neil Halstead,
Sleeping on Roads

Joe Pass, *Virtuoso*

1 We recommend grilling the steak. If you have a barbecue or George Foreman grill, light it or plug it in now. If you don't have either of those, turn on your broiler. Pull the steak out of the fridge to let it come to room temperature.

2 Pour 2 tablespoons oil into the large frying pan and put it on the stove over medium-high heat. When the oil is hot (when it looks runny), add the remaining diced onion and garlic. Cook until the onion looks soft. Add the diced bell pepper and cook for 4 minutes, stirring frequently. Add the corn and black beans and cook for 3 minutes, stirring frequently. Salt and grind in pepper to taste. Cover and reduce the heat to the lowest setting.

3 Wrap the tortillas in foil. If you're using a gas or charcoal grill, place the tortillas on the perimeter of the rack to warm. Otherwise, place them on the lowest oven rack. Dump the tortilla chips into the salad bowl and put them on the table, along with the salsa and guacamole (remove the lime slices from the guac).

4 Cook the steak: If you're grilling, put it on the grill. Otherwise, put it in the small baking pan (discard the marinade that's left behind in the bowl) and slide it in the broiler or, if your broiler is in your oven, put the pan in there, on the top rack. Grilling and broiling times are roughly the same. Ask your lady friend how she likes her steak: For medium-rare, cook for 8 minutes (flip after 4 minutes), or until the thermometer registers 145°F when stuck in the center of the steak; for medium, cook for 10 minutes (flip after 5 minutes), or to 160°F. When it's done, remove it from the heat and extinguish whatever heat source you were using.

5 Cut the steak into ¼" strips and put them on dinner plates. Stir the remaining chopped cilantro into the corny bean mixture, put it in the last clean mixing bowl, and set it on the table. Turn off the stove burner. Pull the warm tortillas off the grill or out of the oven, take them out of the foil, put them on a plate, and serve with everything else.

Tienes hambre? Arriba!

White Meat

What It Really Is:
Chicken, Veggies, and Salad

What You Tell Her It Is:
Breast of Chicken Pan Roasted in Rosemary, Garlic, & White Wine, with Oven-Roasted Potatoes, Parsnips, & Carrots, & Endive-Watercress Salad Topped with Bleu Cheese

Cooking time, from prep to plate:
approximately 90 minutes

Hibernation

Feeling peckish? Turn fowl play into fair game with this gallinaceous horn of good 'n' plenty. Complete with a medley of roasted winter veggies, a sidecar bleu-plate special salad, and a long loaf of bready goodness, this is ideal hibernation food. If you can't stand the red meat, get out the chicken!

Ingredients to Buy

1	bunch Italian (flat-leaf) parsley
2	heads Belgian endive
1	bunch watercress
1	container (4 ounces) crumbled blue cheese
10-12	baby white potatoes
2	long, thin carrots
1	long parsnip
2	bone-in chicken breast halves
1	package fresh rosemary
1	half bottle (375 milliliters) white wine (get a cheapie)
1	can (14 ounces) chicken stock
1	French baguette

You may see blue cheese labeled as BLEU CHEESE. **Don't panic, you're not dyslexic—the French are. However, if you see chicken breasts marked as** NEKCIHC STSAERB, **you have a problem.**

SHOPPING TIP: Parsnips look like albino carrots.

Ingredients You Should Already Have

3 cloves garlic
1 bottle extra virgin olive oil
1 box kosher salt
Millful black peppercorns
1 stick salted butter
1 bottle balsamic vinegar

Kitchen Equipment

Cutting board   Chef's and/or paring knives   Salad bowl   Plastic wrap   2 mixing bowls
Vegetable peeler   Large baking pan   Timer   Large frying pan with lid   Bread knife
3 small plates   Aluminum foil   Meat thermometer   2 dinner plates

1 Set the oven to 400°F. If you will be drinking white wine, put it in the fridge. Warm white wine is gross. Think flat Fresca.

2 Peel the garlic and discard the paper husks. Set aside the naked cloves. Rinse a handful of the parsley and shake it dry. Cut off and discard the stems and finely chop the leaves.

DID YOU KNOW? Belgian endive is grown in total darkness. Exposure to light turns the leaves green and bitter, just like it does to you on a hungover Saturday morning.

3 Make the salad: Get ready to work with some cheese that smells like foot odor. Cut off the butt ends of the endive heads. Peel off and discard the outermost leaves. Slice the heads in half lengthwise. Again cutting lengthwise, cut each half into ⅛"-wide slices. Place the slices in the salad bowl. Rinse the watercress and pat it dry with paper towels. Coarsely chop it and add it to the bowl. Add the blue cheese and toss. Cover the bowl with plastic wrap and put it in the fridge.

4 Get started cooking the veggies: Rinse the potatoes, cut them into quarters, and place them in a mixing bowl. Peel the carrots and parsnip. Cut them into ½" sections and add them to the bowl. Add ¼ cup oil. Lightly salt and grind on pepper. Toss. Dump into the large baking pan. Place the pan on the middle oven rack. The veggies should cook for 40 minutes. Set the timer.

In progress: Wine chilling, salad chilling, veggies roasting
Time remaining: 40 to 50 minutes
Things left to do: Cook chicken, slice bread, dress salad

Get Cooking

1. Get started cooking the chicken: Slice 1 tablespoon butter (tablespoon measurements are indicated on the butter wrapper) and put it in the large frying pan. Put the pan on the stove over medium-high heat. When the butter is melted, add 2 tablespoons oil. When the oil is hot (when it looks runny), add the chicken. Cook for 3 minutes on each side, or until golden brown. Add the garlic and 1 sprig of rosemary. Cook until the garlic turns light gold in color. Lightly salt and grind on pepper. Add 1 cup white wine and ½ cup of the chicken stock. Cook until the wine bubbles, then cook for another 30 seconds. Reduce the heat to low and cover the pan, placing the lid slightly ajar. The chicken will need to cook for 35 to 45 minutes. Watch your time.

2. Slice the baguette, place the pieces in the other mixing bowl, and set on the table. Put the remaining butter on a small plate and set that on the table, too. Give the veggies in the oven a quick stir.

3. When the timer goes off, the veggies should be done. Poke them with a fork to make sure they're tender. Remove the pan from the oven, cover it with foil, and place it on the stovetop to keep warm.

4. Check on the chicken: It's done when a meat thermometer inserted in the thickest portion registers 160°F and the juices run clear. Remove the pan from the heat and turn off the burner.

5. Get the salad out of the fridge and drizzle it with oil and vinegar. Lightly salt and grind on pepper. Toss. Set the bowl on the table.

6. Arrange the chicken and veggies on 2 dinner plates and sprinkle lightly with the chopped parsley. Place a sprig of rosemary on each chicken breast. Spoon the salad onto 2 small plates and serve.

Man, that was easy. Before you head to the table, check to make sure your fly isn't down.

Drink This

S. Quirico Vernaccia di San Gimignano, <$10

Casa Lapostolle Sauvignon Blanc, <$15

Louis Jadot Mâcon-Villages, <$15

Play This

Bob Dylan, *Nashville Skyline*

The Jimmy Giuffre 3, *The Jimmy Giuffre 3*

Van Morrison, *Astral Weeks*

What It Really Is:
Chicken-and-Veggie Stir-Fry with Rice

What You Tell Her It Is:
Stir-Fried Chicken & Mixed Garden Vegetables with Fresh Mint & Basil, Served on a Bed of Sticky Rice

Cooking time, from prep to plate:
approximately 60 minutes

Hot and Bothered

Cause a stir with this frying-pan pan-Asian garden of earthly delights. Watch as some drunken chicken breasts get all hot and bothered and share a bed of rice with an all-star cast of yummies. Even comes with a built-in breath freshener.

Ingredients to Buy

1	bottle dry sherry
1	pound boneless, skinless chicken breast halves
1	piece fresh ginger (approximately 2" long)
1	small yellow onion
1	small red bell pepper
2	long, thin carrots
1	small head broccoli
1	bunch scallions
1	bunch fresh basil
1	bunch fresh mint
1	bag sushi rice
1	package sliced fresh button mushrooms
2	handfuls bean sprouts
2	ounces toasted sesame seeds

DID YOU KNOW? Ginger has been used for centuries to fight colds. Chinese herbalists believe that it promotes sweating and thereby flushes toxins from the body.

If you're like us, you probably get sushi confused with yoga.

If you can't find sesame seeds in your supermarket, ask a stock boy, "Can you tell me how to get . . . how to get to sesame seeds?"

Ingredients You Should Already Have

1 bottle soy sauce
1 bottle toasted sesame oil
2 cloves garlic
1 box kosher salt

Kitchen Equipment

2 mixing bowls   Whisk   Cutting board   Chef's and/or paring knives   Strainer
Small saucepan with lid   Large frying pan   3 dinner plates

This marinade is also effective as a depilatory.

1 If you will be drinking white wine, put it in the fridge.

2 Marinate the chicken: In a mixing bowl, combine 2 tablespoons dry sherry and 2 tablespoons soy sauce. Whisk in 1 tablespoon sesame oil. Plop the chicken on the cutting board then cut away and discard any tendon remnants and yellowish fatty tissue. Cut the chicken into 1" cubes and add it to the bowl. Toss and put in the fridge. Wash the cutting board thoroughly with hot and soapy water before proceeding.

3 With the paring knife, remove and discard the skin from the ginger. Finely dice the ginger and set it aside. Peel the garlic and discard the paper husks. Finely dice the garlic and set aside.

4 Cut off the top and bottom of the onion, then peel off and discard the skin. Cut the onion into quarters and chop each quarter into 3 pieces. Put the onion in the other mixing bowl. Cut the pepper in half, then remove and discard the stem and seeds. Slice the pepper into 1" squares and add them to the bowl. Peel the carrots, slice them in half lengthwise, and cut them into ½" chunks. Add them to the bowl.

5 Rinse the broccoli. Chop off and discard the main stem. Cut the remaining head into bite-size miniheads. (Your lady friend might call these *florets*.) Set aside. Rinse and shake dry the scallions. Cut off and discard the roots. Starting from the root end, cut the bottom 5" of each scallion into thin, round slices. Set aside.

6 Stack 6 large basil leaves and roll them lengthwise (like you would roll a cigarette). Cut the roll crosswise into thin slices. Repeat with another 6 leaves. Repeat with 12 mint leaves. When you have 3 tablespoons of each, set them aside.

In progress: Wine chilling, chicken soaking
Time remaining: 20 to 25 minutes
Things left to do: Cook rice, fry chicken and veggies

Get
Cooking

1 Make the rice: Pour 1¼ cups rice into the strainer. Swish around under cold running water until the water runs clear. Shake off excess water. Pour 1¼ cups water into the small saucepan. Add the rinsed rice and a pinch of salt. Cover and place the pan on the stove over high heat. When the water starts to boil, reduce the heat to the lowest setting. Let the rice simmer for 15 minutes, then turn off the heat. Leave the pan covered and continue with step 2.

2 Get started stir-frying: Pour 2 tablespoons sesame oil into the large frying pan (or into a wok if you happen to own one) and put it on the stove over high heat. When the oil is hot (when it looks runny), add the chicken. Cook for 2 to 3 minutes, stirring frequently. Remove the chicken from the pan and place it on a dinner plate.

3 Continue stir-frying: Pour another 2 tablespoons sesame oil into the same frying pan and reduce the heat to medium-high. When the oil is hot, add the onion, pepper, and carrots. Cook for 1 minute. Stir. Add the garlic and 2 tablespoons ginger. Stir. Add the broccoli and mushrooms. Cook for 4 to 6 minutes, stirring frequently. Add the chicken and 2 tablespoons soy sauce. Cook for 3 to 5 minutes, stirring frequently. Add 2 tablespoons of the basil, 2 tablespoons of the mint, and the bean sprouts. Give it all a quick stir and then remove it from the heat. Turn off the burner.

4 Put a mound of the rice on each of 2 dinner plates. Spoon the stir-fry over the mounds. Sprinkle with the scallions, sesame seeds, and the remaining 1 tablespoon basil and 1 tablespoon mint.

Serve it like Andre Agassi.

Drink This

Joh. Jos. Prüm Riesling Kabinett, <$10

Pierre Sparr Gewürztraminer *Carte d'Or*, <$15

Beer of your choice

Play This

Billie Holiday, *Lady Day: The Best of Billie Holiday*

Massive Attack, *Blue Lines*

Youssou N'Dour, *The Guide (Wommat)*

What It Really Is:

Pork, Cornmeal Mush, and Tomatoes

What You Tell Her It Is:

Garlic-Rosemary Pork Tenderloin with Creamy Gorgonzola Polenta & Pesto-Baked Tomatoes

Cooking time, from prep to plate:
approximately 60 minutes

Tender

Gird your loins, unbutton your lip, and untie your tongue—there's a party in your mouth and everyone's invited! There are tender, lean tenderloins of moist porkiness, riddled with garlic land mines that explode with flavor. There's a creamy cornmeal concoction providing the ideal vehicle for stinky cheese, and some peppy Parmesanian pestomato poppers. Whether she eats like a bird or like a horse, she'll be eating out of your hand.

Ingredients to Buy

1½   pounds pork tenderloin
1   package fresh rosemary
4   Roma (plum) tomatoes
1   container (8 ounces) prepared pesto
1   container (8 ounces) freshly grated
      Parmesan cheese
1   half bottle (375 milliliters) white wine
      (get a cheapie)
1   can (14½ ounces) chicken broth
1   box polenta mix
4   ounces Gorgonzola cheese

Fresh rosemary looks like pine needles. Make sure your rosemary is not, in fact, pine needles.

SHOPPING TIP: Polenta mix can usually be found in the same supermarket aisle as flour.

DID YOU KNOW? For some reason, the London Stock Exchange is nicknamed Gorgonzola Hall.

Ingredients You Should Already Have

3 cloves garlic
1 box kosher salt
1 teaspoon fresh ground + millful black
   peppercorns
1 bottle extra virgin olive oil

Kitchen Equipment

Cutting board   Chef's and/or paring knives   Mixing bowl   Small baking pan   Large baking pan
Large frying pan   Aluminum foil   Timer   Medium saucepan   Meat thermometer   2 dinner plates

Pork marketing-campaign idea: tagline "Got pork?" supporting print advertising featuring various celebrities sporting pork moustaches.

1 Set the oven to 400°F.

2 Season the pork: Peel the garlic and discard the paper husks. Slice the garlic into paper-thin slivers. Cut deep slits all over the pork and insert a sliver into each. Remove the needles from 4 sprigs of rosemary and discard the stems. Chop the needles as finely as possible and put them in the mixing bowl. Add 1 teaspoon salt and 1 teaspoon pepper and mix thoroughly. Add the pork and rub it with the seasoning, coating the meat as evenly as possible. Put the pork in the small baking pan and set aside.

3 Rinse the tomatoes and slice them in half lengthwise. Scoop out and discard about half of the insides. Fill each tomato with pesto, top with Parmesan, and put faceup on the large baking pan. Set aside.

In progress: Pork and tomatoes waiting
Time remaining: 35 to 40 minutes
Things left to do: Cook pork, make polenta, bake tomatoes

Get Cooking

1 Get started cooking the pork: Pour 2 tablespoons oil into the large frying pan and put it on the stove over medium-high heat. When the oil is hot (when it looks runny), add the pork and cook until brown on each side (1 to 2 minutes per side). Put the pork back in the small baking pan. Add 1 cup white wine and 1 cup chicken broth. Cover the pan with foil and put it on the middle oven rack. Set the timer to 30 minutes.

2 When the pork has been in the oven for 20 minutes, put the pan of tomatoes on the top oven rack. Cook the tomatoes for 10 minutes.

3 In the medium saucepan, cook 2 servings of polenta, following the directions on the box. Cut the Gorgonzola into 5 pieces. As the polenta thickens, stir in the Gorgonzola, mixing thoroughly. Salt and grind on pepper to taste.

4 Check on the pork: When the timer goes off, insert the thermometer into the center. If it registers 160°F and the juices run clear, the pork is done, and you can remove it from the oven. Let it sit for 5 minutes. By now, the tomatoes should also be done. Remove them from the oven, too. Then turn off the oven.

5 Spoon the polenta onto 2 dinner plates. Slice the pork into 1"-thick medallions and arrange on the plates. Place the tomatoes alongside the polenta and pork.

Dig in and pig out.

Drink This

Casa Lapostolle
Sauvignon Blanc, <$10

Conde de Valdemar
Crianza Rioja, <$15

Guigal **Côtes du Rhône,** <$15

Play This

Tim Buckley, *Happy Sad*

Various Artists, *Brazil Classics, Vol. 1: Beleza Tropical*

Paul Weller, *Paul Weller*

What It Really Is:
Chicken, Couscous, Zucchini, and Salad

What You Tell Her It Is:
Lemon-&-Thyme-Infused Baked Breast of Chicken with Couscous, Sautéed Courgettes, & Greek Salad

Cooking time, from prep to plate:
approximately 90 minutes

Herbage

When life hands you lemons, make . . . Lemon-Thyme Chicken! This *poulet de campagne*, also known as Chicken Spicoli, is under the influence of some serious herbage. Turn yourself into a tastemaker with a Mediterranean-style feast for the ages that doesn't take ages to make.

Ingredients to Buy

1	pound boneless, skinless chicken breasts
3	lemons
1	yellow onion
1	shallot
1	package fresh thyme
4	Roma (plum) tomatoes
1	hothouse cucumber
1	red onion
1	container (12 ounces) crumbled feta cheese
1	long, thin zucchini
1	head butter lettuce
1	box garlic–olive oil couscous mix

Pick the breasts that look the perkiest.

SHOPPING TIP: Hothouse cukes are long and thin, and they usually come shrink-wrapped. Like most guys, you'll probably feel weird about buying a long, sheathed cucumber. Just bury it at the bottom of your shopping cart.

If you can't find butter lettuce, buy I Can't Believe It's Not Butter lettuce.

SHOPPING TIP: Couscous is a pasta and is found near the rice at the supermarket.

Ingredients You Should Already Have

8 cloves garlic
1 bottle extra virgin olive oil
1 box kosher salt
Millful black peppercorns
1 bottle red wine vinegar
1 stick salted butter

Kitchen Equipment

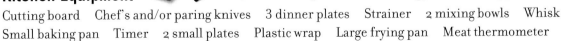

Cutting board   Chef's and/or paring knives   3 dinner plates   Strainer   2 mixing bowls   Whisk
Small baking pan   Timer   2 small plates   Plastic wrap   Large frying pan   Meat thermometer

1 Set the oven to 350°F. If you will be drinking white wine, put it in the fridge.

2 Plop the chicken on the cutting board, then cut away and discard any tendon remnants and yellowish fatty tissue. Think of this as chicken lipo-suction or chicken breast reduction. Set aside the breasts on one of the dinner plates. Wash the cutting board thoroughly with hot and soapy water—you'll need it for chopping up other ingredients, and you don't want the other stuff to get raw-chicken cooties.

3 Make the marinade for the chicken: Set the strainer in a mixing bowl. Cut 2 of the lemons in half and, holding them above the strainer, squeeze the juice out of them. Discard the rinds, seeds, and pulp. Cut the tops off the yellow onion and the shallot. Peel off and discard the skins. Slice each into circular cross sections (like you would put on hamburgers). Add the onion to the bowl and set aside the shallot. Peel the garlic and discard the paper husks. Dice finely and add half to the bowl. Set aside the remaining garlic. Remove the leaves from the thyme stems. Discard the stems and finely chop the leaves. Set aside 2 tablespoons of the chopped thyme and add the remainder to the bowl. Whisk in $^3/_4$ cup oil. Lightly salt and grind on pepper. Add the chicken and flip to coat both sides. Put the bowl in the fridge for 30 to 40 minutes.

4 Start on the salad: Rinse the tomatoes, then cut off and discard the stem ends. Peel the cucumber, then cut off and discard the ends. Chop the tomatoes and cucumber into ½" cubes and put them in the other mixing bowl. Cut off the top of the red onion. Peel off and discard the skin. Cut the onion into thin slices and add them to the bowl. Set the strainer in the bowl. Cut the remaining lemon in half, hold the halves over the strainer, and squeeze out the juice. Discard the rinds, seeds, and pulp. Remove the strainer from the bowl. Add the feta, the remaining 2 tablespoons of thyme, 1 tablespoon red wine vinegar, and a dash of oil to the bowl. Lightly salt and grind on pepper. Mix thoroughly and set aside.

5 Rinse the zucchini, then cut off and discard the ends. Slice the rest into ¼"-thick disks. Set aside.

When the chicken has soaked for at least 30 minutes, continue with "Get Cooking" step 1.

In progress: Wine chilling, chicken soaking, salad and zucchini waiting
Time remaining: 30 to 40 minutes
Things left to do: Bake chicken, finish salad, make couscous, cook zucchini

DID YOU KNOW? Feta cheese can be made from the milk of goats, sheep, or cows. Crumbled feta resembles the current state of the Acropolis.

69

1. Cook the chicken: Pull it out of the fridge, remove it from the marinade, and place it in the small baking pan. Discard the marinade. Place the baking pan on the middle oven rack. Set the timer to 25 minutes.

2. Finish the salad: Tear off 4 large, good-looking leaves from the head of butter lettuce. Rinse the leaves and pat them dry with a paper towel. Place 2 of the leaves rounded side down on each of the 2 small plates. Spoon on the salad mixture. Cover with plastic wrap and put the plates in the fridge.

3. Cook the couscous according to the directions on the box.

4. Put ¼ stick of butter in the large frying pan and melt it on the stove over medium heat. Add the sliced shallot and the remaining chopped garlic. Cook, stirring, until the shallot looks soft. Add the zucchini and cook, stirring frequently, for 2 to 3 minutes. Turn off the burner. Lightly salt and grind on pepper.

5. Back to the chicken: When the timer goes off, insert the thermometer in the thickest portion. If it registers 160°F and the juices run clear, the chicken is done, and you can remove it from the oven. Don't forget to turn off the oven.

6. Fluff the couscous with a fork and put a mound on the center of each clean dinner plate. Place a chicken breast on top of each mound and arrange zucchini on either side. Get the salads out of the fridge.

Go to table. Go directly to table. Do not pass GO. Do not pass gas.

Drink This

S. Quirico Vernaccia
di San Gimignano, <$10

Louis Jadot
Mâcon-Villages, <$15

Adelsheim Pinot Gris, $15+

Play This

Everything but the Girl,
Amplified Heart

Thelonious Monk, *Thelonious
Alone in San Francisco*

Talk Talk,
The Colour of Spring

What It Really Is:

Turkey, Green Beans, Salad, and Bread

What You Tell Her It Is:

Balsamic-Marinated Turkey Breast, Spicy Garlic French Beans, Tomato-Avocado–Red Onion Salad, & French Baguette

Cooking time, from prep to plate: approximately 60 minutes

Vibrations

What foods these morsels be! Here's a sultry poultry dish courtesy of the "other" Other White Meat. Evoking the good vibrations of California cuisine, this is a healthy, wealthy, and wise thinner-dinner that would make Richard Simmons weep with delight. Fortunately, it's not him you've invited over.

Ingredients to Buy

2	boneless turkey breasts (about ½ pound each)
2	handfuls French green beans
3	vine-ripened tomatoes
1	avocado
1	lemon
1	small red onion
1	French baguette
1	bottle red pepper flakes

French green beans are very thin. American green beans are fatter. When shopping, picture French and American people and this will not be hard to remember.

DID YOU KNOW? The word *avocado* is derived from the Nahuatl word *ahuacatl*, which literally means "testicle."

Red onions are actually purple. The confusion caused by this misnomer is responsible for most produce-aisle pileups.

Ingredients You Should Already Have

6 cloves garlic
1 bottle balsamic vinegar
1 jar Dijon mustard
1 bottle extra virgin olive oil
1 box kosher salt
Millful black peppercorns
1 stick salted butter

Kitchen Equipment

Cutting board   Chef's and/or paring knives   2 mixing bowls   Whisk   Strainer   3 dinner plates
Plastic wrap   Small baking pan   Timer   Bread knife   3 small plates   Large frying pan
Meat thermometer

1 Set the oven to 400°F. If you will be drinking white wine, put it in the fridge.

2 Make the marinade for the turkey: Peel the garlic and discard the paper husks. Finely dice. In a mixing bowl, combine ½ cup vinegar, 2 tablespoons mustard, and half of the garlic. Set aside the rest of the garlic. Whisk ½ cup oil into the marinade. Lightly salt and grind in pepper. Mix thoroughly.

3 Add the turkey breasts to the bowl and flip to coat both sides. Put the bowl in the fridge.

4 Put the beans in the strainer and rinse. Snap off and discard the stems. Set aside the beans.

5 Rinse the tomatoes and cut them into wedges (as you would cut apples). Cut out and discard the stems and cores. Set aside the wedges.

6 Cut the avocado into quarters (as you would cut a pear). Remove and discard the pit. Peel off and discard the skin. Cut the quarters lengthwise into ¼"-thick slices. Cut the lemon in half and, holding the halves over the strainer, squeeze the juice over the avocado. Discard the rinds, seeds, and pulp. Set aside the lemony avocado.

7 Cut off the top of the onion. Peel off and discard the skin. Slice half of the onion into circular cross sections (like you would put on hamburgers). Set aside.

8 Get started making the salad: On a dinner plate, arrange the tomato and avocado slices in a radial fan formation, alternating tomato, avocado, tomato, avocado, et cetera. Separate the onion slices into rings and lay them over the top. Cover the plate with plastic wrap and put it in the fridge.

In progress: Wine chilling, turkey soaking, salad chilling, beans waiting

Time remaining: 30 to 35 minutes

Things left to do: Bake turkey, slice bread, dress salad, sauté beans

Get Cooking

1 Start cooking the turkey: Get it out of the fridge, place it in the small baking pan, and pour on the marinade. Place the pan on the middle oven rack. Set the timer to 25 minutes. Take the next few minutes to set the table and work on your jump shot.

2 Slice the baguette and place the slices in the other mixing bowl. Set the bowl on the table. Put the butter on a small plate and set that on the table, too.

3 Dress the salad: Get it out of the fridge and drizzle it with oil and vinegar. Lightly salt and grind on pepper. Set the plate on the table, along with 2 small plates for serving.

4 Cook the beans: Pour 2 tablespoons oil into the large frying pan and put it on the stove over medium heat. When the oil is hot (when it looks runny), add the remaining garlic and cook, stirring, for 1 minute. Add the beans and stir. Add 1 tablespoon water and 1 teaspoon red pepper flakes. Cook, stirring, for 3 minutes, being careful not to let the garlic burn. Cover the pan and turn off the burner.

5 When the timer goes off, check on the turkey: It's done when a thermometer inserted into the thickest portion registers 170°F and the juices run clear. Remove it from the oven. Don't forget to turn off the oven.

6 Slice each turkey breast into 1"-thick medallions and fan the pieces out on a dinner plate. Arrange some beans on both sides of the turkey.

Cook no further. Sit down and eat up.

Drink This

La Vieille Ferme
Côtes du Ventoux, <$10

Louis Jadot Bourgogne
Pinot Noir, <$15

Casa Lapostolle
Sauvignon Blanc, <$15

Play This

Air, *Moon Safari*

Bee Gees, *Best of Bee Gees*

The Left Banke,
There's Gonna Be a Storm

What It Really Is:
Pork Chops, Green Beans, Salad, and Bread

What You Tell Her It Is:
Garlic-Infused Pork Chops, Sautéed Haricots Verts & Button Mushrooms, Spinach Chef's Salad with Raspberry Vinaigrette, & French Baguette

Cooking time, from prep to plate:
approximately 90 minutes

Double Shot

Attention, pork fans! Here's a double shot of the good stuff ("the good stuff" = pork) and more fungus than you can shake a stick at. Toss in some plant parts and a couple of delectables from your grocer's dairy case, and next thing you know, you're knocking back bacon and eggs for dinner. What's more, it's easy like Sunday morning.

Ingredients to Buy

2	portobello mushrooms
½	dozen eggs
½	pound bacon
2	bone-in pork chops (¾ pound each)
1	container garlic salt
1	bag prewashed baby spinach
1	container (8 ounces) crumbled feta cheese
1	bottle raspberry vinegar
2	handfuls French green beans
1	pound sliced fresh button mushrooms
1	French baguette

Get chops with a bone to pick.

The next time you're plotting revenge, bear in mind that the only thing worse than salt in the wounds is garlic salt in the wounds.

Warning: Feta is a "gateway cheese" and may lead to the heavier stuff.

DID YOU KNOW? Vinegar was once used as a hair conditioner.

Ingredients You Should Already Have

1 bottle balsamic vinegar

1 jar Dijon mustard

1 box kosher salt

Millful black peppercorns

1 bottle extra virgin olive oil

1 stick salted butter

Kitchen Equipment

Cutting board Chef's and/or paring knives 3 mixing bowls Whisk Small baking pan
Medium saucepan Strainer Cereal bowl Large frying pan with lid Large baking pan
Salad bowl Plastic wrap 3 small plates Bread knife Meat thermometer 2 dinner plates

Contrary to popular belief, portobello is not an Italian suitcase company. And a baguette is not a small bag.

1 Turn on your broiler. If you will be drinking white wine, put it in the fridge.

2 Marinate the portobellos: With a paper towel, carefully remove any loose dirt from the tops of them, then cut off and discard the stems. In a mixing bowl, combine ½ cup balsamic vinegar and 2 tablespoons mustard. Lightly salt and grind in pepper. Whisk in ¼ cup oil. Add the portobellos and flip to coat evenly. Place them gill side up in the small baking pan and spoon marinade over the gills.

3 Fill the medium saucepan half full of water and put it on the stove over high heat. When the water is rapidly boiling, carefully lower 2 eggs into the pan with a large spoon. Set aside the other 4 eggs for tomorrow's breakfast. Boil the 2 eggs for 10 minutes. Pour them into the strainer to drain and then place them in a cereal bowl of cold water. Set the bowl aside.

Do not pour the bacon grease down the drain. Bacon grease does to plumbing what it does to arteries. Pour it into an empty can, let it solidify, and then discard it, can and all.

4 Put the large frying pan on the stove over medium-high heat. Add the bacon and fry until well-done, 7 to 10 minutes. Frying bacon is kind of like a grease volcano. Beware airborne molten fat. When the bacon is done, put it on layered paper towels. Wash the frying pan; you'll need to use it again, for the beans.

5 Put the pan of portobellos in the broiler or, if your broiler is in your oven, put the pan in there, on the top rack. Cook for 3 minutes on each side. Remove the pan from the broiler and set it aside to cool.

6 Place the pork chops in the large baking pan. Grind pepper onto both sides. Sprinkle both sides with garlic salt. Set aside.

7 Make the salad: Open the bag of spinach and dump the leaves into the salad bowl. With your fingers, crumble the bacon over the spinach. Slice the portobellos into thin strips and add them to the bowl. Remove the shells from the eggs and discard. Cut the eggs into thin slices and place them on top of the salad. Sprinkle the feta over the salad. Cover the bowl with plastic wrap and put it in the fridge.

8 Make the salad dressing: In the second mixing bowl, combine $\frac{1}{4}$ cup raspberry vinegar and 2 tablespoons mustard. Lightly salt and grind in pepper. Whisk in $\frac{1}{4}$ cup oil. Set aside.

In progress: Wine chilling, pork waiting, salad chilling
Time remaining: 30 to 40 minutes
Things left to do: Boil and sauté beans, broil pork chops, dress salad, slice bread

1 Get started cooking the beans: Fill the medium saucepan $\frac{3}{4}$ full of water and put it on the stove over medium-high heat. Rinse the beans in the strainer. Snap off and discard the stems. When the pan of water is boiling, add the beans and cook for $1\frac{1}{2}$ to 2 minutes. Turn off the heat and pour the beans into the strainer to drain. Rinse them with cold water and set them aside.

2 Get started cooking the pork: Place the pan of chops in the broiler or on the middle oven rack. Cook for 8 to 10 minutes on each side. Keep an eye on the clock.

3 Finish the beans: Put the large frying pan on the stove over medium-high heat. Add 2 tablespoons oil. When the oil is hot (when it looks runny), add the button mushrooms. Cook, stirring frequently, for 3 to 5 minutes, until soft. Add the green beans and cook for $1\frac{1}{2}$ to 2 minutes. Lightly salt and grind on pepper. Turn off the burner and cover the pan to keep the veggies warm. If you haven't flipped the pork, do so now.

4 Dress the salad: Get it out of the fridge. Mix the salad dressing thoroughly and then pour it over the salad. Toss. Set it on the table with 2 of the small plates for serving.

5 Slice the baguette and place the slices in the third mixing bowl. Set the bowl on the table. Put the butter on the third small plate and set that on the table, too.

6 Check on the pork chops: When they've cooked for 8 to 10 minutes on each side, insert the thermometer in the center of a chop. If it registers 160°F and the juices run clear, the pork is done, and you can remove it from the broiler and turn off the heat.

7 Arrange each chop on a dinner plate, along with the beans and mushrooms.

Kudos. Don't go changin'. Unless, of course, you got some stuff on your pants back in step 3.

Drink This

Firesteed Pinot Noir, <$10

Louis Jadot Bourgogne Pinot Noir, <$15

Trimbach Pinot Blanc, <$15

Play This

Lloyd Cole, *Love Story*

Miles Davis, *Porgy and Bess*

Tom Waits, *Closing Time*

Sea Meat

What It Really Is:
Tuna, Rice, Veggies, and Cucumber Salad

What You Tell Her It Is:
Sesame-Encrusted Ahi Tuna, Stir-Fried Shiitake Mushrooms & Asparagus, & Cucumber-Sesame Salad

**Cooking time, from prep to plate:
approximately 60 minutes**

Harmonious

This Asian equation is a can't-miss recipe for success whereby the meatiest of all fishes undergoes a superlative sesame suffusion. The star fish shares the stage with a most harmonious produce-aisle quartet. Open wide and say, "Ahi."

Ingredients to Buy

1	bag sushi rice
2	fresh ahi tuna steaks ($^3/_4$ pound each)
1	bunch scallions
1	hothouse cucumber
1	bottle rice wine vinegar
8	ounces toasted sesame seeds
$^1/_2$	pound shiitake mushrooms
1	bunch asparagus

DID YOU KNOW? Ahi (or yellowfin) tuna can swim at speeds of up to 50 mph and are found in all of the earth's oceans and seas except the Mediterranean.

All right, we know what you're thinking, but it's pronounced "shee-TAH-kay."

Ingredients You Should Already Have

1 bottle soy sauce
1 box kosher salt
1 bottle toasted sesame oil

Kitchen Equipment

Strainer   Mixing bowl   Cutting board   Chef's and/or paring knives   Vegetable peeler   Salad bowl
Plastic wrap   3 dinner plates   Small saucepan with lid   Timer   2 large frying pans

1 If you will be drinking white wine, put it in the fridge.

2 Pour 1¼ cups rice into the strainer. Swish it around under cold running water until the water runs clear. Shake off the excess water and set aside.

3 Marinate the tuna: Put it into the mixing bowl and add 1 cup soy sauce. Set it aside. While it's soaking, point at it and sing "We Will Rock You" into the cucumber. No, really, don't do that.

4 Rinse and shake dry the scallions. Cut off and discard the roots. Starting from the root end, cut the bottom 5" of each scallion into thin, round slices. Set aside.

5 Make the salad: Peel the cucumber, then cut off and discard the ends. Slice the cuke into CD-thin disks. Place the disks in the salad bowl. Pour in ½ cup rice wine vinegar and lightly salt. Sprinkle with half of the sliced scallions. Lightly drizzle with sesame oil. Lightly sprinkle with some of the sesame seeds. Set aside the rest of the seeds. Cover the bowl with plastic wrap and put it in the fridge.

6 Remove the stems from the mushrooms and discard. With a paper towel, brush any dirt off the mushroom caps. Cut each cap into 4 slices. Set aside.

7 Rinse the asparagus, then cut off and discard the butts (the bottom 1" to 2"). Cut each spear diagonally into 3 sections. Set aside.

8 Spread some more of the sesame seeds on a dinner plate, setting aside a few tablespoons' worth. Place the tuna on the seeds and flip to evenly coat the top, bottom, and sides of each steak. Shove the tuna in your pants and do 20 jumping jacks to help season it. No, really, don't do that.

In progress: Wine chilling, salad chilling, tuna and asparagus waiting
Time remaining: 20 to 25 minutes
Things left to do: Cook rice, fry asparagus and mushrooms, fry tuna

Get Cooking

1 Make the rice: Pour 1¼ cups water into the small saucepan. Add a pinch of salt and the rinsed rice. Put on the lid and place the pan on the stove over high heat. When the water is boiling, reduce the heat to the lowest setting. Simmer for 15 minutes. Set the timer and continue with step 2. When the timer goes off after 15 minutes, turn off the heat but leave the rice covered.

2 Get started cooking the veggies: Pour 2 tablespoons sesame oil into a large frying pan. Put the pan on the stove over medium-high heat. When the oil is hot (when it looks runny), add the asparagus and mushrooms. Cook for 3 minutes, stirring frequently. Stir in 1 tablespoon soy sauce and sprinkle with most of the reserved sesame seeds. Reduce the heat to the lowest setting.

3 Get started cooking the tuna: Pour 2 tablespoons sesame oil into the other large frying pan. Put the pan on the stove over medium-high heat. When the oil is hot, add the tuna and cook for 2 to 3 minutes on each side, until rare or medium-rare, respectively. While the tuna is cooking, give the asparagus and mushrooms a quick stir.

4 When the tuna is done, sprinkle it with the remaining half of the scallions.

5 Fluff the rice with a fork. Turn off any and all burners. Get the cucumber salad out of the fridge. Place a scoop of rice on each of the 2 clean dinner plates. Lay the tuna against the rice, and put veggies on the sides of each plate. Sprinkle the remaining reserved sesame seeds over everything.

Your kung fu is no good. Fortunately, your tuna is. Get after it.

Drink This

Trimbach Pinot Blanc, <$15

Pierre Sparr Gewürztraminer *Carte d'Or*, <$15

Louis Jadot Bourgogne Pinot Noir, <$15

Play This

Bill Evans Trio, *Sunday at the Village Vanguard*

Milton Nascimento and Lô Borges, *Clube Da Esquina*

Roxy Music, *Avalon*

What It Really Is:
Salmon, Couscous, Peas, and Salad

What You Tell Her It Is:
Baked Salmon with Creamy Dill Sauce, Garlic Couscous, Blanched Snow Peas, & Garden Salad with Bleu Cheese

Cooking time, from prep to plate:
approximately 60 minutes

Killa

Why swim upstream? The flaky, bakey art of salmon preparation is as easy as getting a MasterCard and more rewarding than its frequent-flier program. These things that make you go "Mmm" are all killa, no filla. So get out your CO-ED BAKED SALMON T-shirt and go with the flow! She'll go for it cook, wine, and sinker.

Ingredients to Buy

3	lemons
1	bunch fresh dill
1¼	pounds skinless salmon fillet
2	handfuls snow peas
1	bag prewashed mesclun salad mix
1	box cherry tomatoes
1	container (4 ounces) crumbled blue cheese
1	container (8 ounces) sour cream
1	box garlic–olive oil couscous mix

Snow peas are harvested with a snow pea plow.

Couscous is to the Middle East as _____ is to Japan.
(a) rice
(b) flan
(c) Wang Chung
(d) windsurfer

Ingredients You Should Already Have

1 box kosher salt
Millful white peppercorns
1 jar Dijon mustard
1 bottle extra virgin olive oil

Kitchen Equipment

Cutting board   Chef's and/or paring knives   Large baking pan   Salad bowl   Plastic wrap
Mixing bowl   Whisk   Timer   Small saucepan   Medium saucepan with lid   2 small plates
2 dinner plates

1 Set the oven to 350°F. If you will be drinking white wine, put it in the fridge.

2 Cut off and discard the ends of the lemons. Cut 1 of the lemons in half. Cut another one into 6 circular slices. Reserve the third for later. Set aside all of them for now.

3 Chop the dill very finely until you have a little more than 4 tablespoons' worth. Set aside.

4 Prep the salmon: Rinse it in cold water and pat it dry with a paper towel. Place it dark side down in the large baking pan. Squeeze the juice of 1 of the lemon halves over the fish. Remove any seeds and lightly salt and grind on pepper. Sprinkle 2 tablespoons of the chopped dill over the fish. Set aside the rest of the dill. Cover the fish with the 6 lemon slices. Set aside.

5 Grab the stem of each snow pea pod and peel the string off the top. Discard the strings. Set aside the pods.

Since they can make cherry-size tomatoes, you'd think they could make tomato-size cherries.

6 Make the salad: Open the bag of mesclun mix and dump the greens into the salad bowl. Rinse the cherry tomatoes and pat them dry with paper towels. Cut them in half and sprinkle them over the greens. Add the blue cheese and toss. Cover the bowl with plastic wrap and put it in the fridge.

7 Make the sauce for the salmon: In the mixing bowl, combine the sour cream, 2 tablespoons of the chopped dill, and 2 tablespoons mustard. Squeeze in the juice of the other lemon half. Remove any seeds and whisk thoroughly. (Mixing sour cream too vigorously can result in an affliction called sour elbow.) Salt and grind in pepper to taste. Cover the bowl with plastic wrap and put it in the fridge.

In progress: Wine chilling, salmon waiting, peas and salad waiting, dill sauce chilling

Time remaining: 20 to 30 minutes

Things left to do: Bake salmon, cook couscous, boil peas, dress salad

Get Cooking

1 Get started cooking the salmon: Put the pan on the middle oven rack. The salmon will need to cook for 20 to 25 minutes. Set the timer.

2 In the small saucepan, cook the couscous, following the directions on the box.

3 Cook the snow peas: Fill the medium saucepan half full of water and bring to a boil over medium-high heat. Add the snow peas. Cook for 1½ to 2 minutes, until bright green. Turn off the burner. Pour the snow peas into the strainer to drain. Return them to the pan. Drizzle with olive oil. Lightly salt and grind on pepper. Toss. Cover with the pan's lid to keep warm.

4 Check on the salmon: When the timer goes off, see whether the fish is opaque orange and firm to the touch. If not, return it to the oven for another 3 to 5 minutes. When done, remove it from the oven and cut it in half. Don't forget to turn off the oven.

5 Dress the salad: Drizzle it with olive oil, sprinkle lightly with salt, toss well, and set it on the table, with 2 small plates for serving.

6 Fluff the couscous with a fork, then place some on each of the dinner plates. Also arrange the salmon and snow peas on the plates. Turn off any burners. Get the dill sauce out of the fridge and put a small dollop on each fillet. Lightly sprinkle with the remaining chopped dill. Cut the remaining lemon into quarters and put two on each plate for squeezing over fish.

You've just turned a raw deal into a done deal. Enjoy.

Drink This

Louis Jadot **Bourgogne Pinot Noir,** <**$15**

Trimbach **Pinot Blanc,** <**$15**

Adelsheim **Pinot Gris, $15+**

Play This

Francis Dunnery, *Man*

Duke Ellington and His Orchestra, . . . *And His Mother Called Him Bill*

Richard Hawley, *Late Night Final*

What It Really Is:

Lobster, Asparagus, Potatoes, and Bread

What You Tell Her It Is:

Steamed Lobster Tail with Drawn Butter, Steamed Asparagus, Baby Red Potatoes with Fresh Dill, & French Baguette Topped with Sautéed Button Mushrooms

Cooking time, from prep to plate:
approximately 60 minutes

Titillated

Sheer ambrosia! Here's a butter bomb that will make your tongue feel like break-dancing and have your arteries cowering in horror—a feast to tell your grandkids about and to lie to your doctor about. Try this at home: She'll be titillated.

Ingredients to Buy

10-12	baby red potatoes
1	bunch fresh Italian (flat-leaf) parsley
1	bunch fresh dill
2	lemons
1	bunch asparagus
1	French baguette
1	pound sliced fresh button mushrooms
1	half bottle (375 milliliters) white wine (get a cheapie)
2	lobster tails (about ½ pound each)

Red potatoes are cute when they're babies. Once they hit puberty, they're a nightmare.

SHOPPING TIP: If you can't find sliced button mushrooms in the produce aisle, buy whole mushrooms and slice them into slivers as you get started with the prep.

Lobster: giving bottom feeders a good name. DID YOU KNOW? In the late 1800s, lobster was so abundant that it was used as bait.

Ingredients You Should Already Have

1 bottle extra virgin olive oil
1 box kosher salt
Millful + 1 tablespoon black peppercorns
4 cloves garlic
1 stick salted butter

Kitchen Equipment

Cutting board   Chef's and/or paring knives   Large baking pan   Aluminum foil   Stockpot
Bread knife   2 mixing bowls   2 dinner plates   Large frying pan   Medium saucepan   Timer
Strainer   Scissors   2 cereal bowls

1 Set the oven to 400°F. If you will be drinking white wine, put it in the fridge.

2 Start the potatoes: Scrub them under cold running water and pat them dry with paper towels. Cut them into quarters. Put them in the large baking pan. Drizzle with oil and toss to coat. Lightly salt and grind on pepper. Cover with foil and place on the middle oven rack. (If you have fillings or braces, do not chew on the aluminum foil.) The potatoes will need to bake for 30 to 40 minutes. Note the time and continue with steps 3 through 7.

3 Rinse the parsley and shake dry. Cut off and discard the stems. Finely chop the leaves until you have 4 tablespoons parsley. Set aside. Finely chop 4 tablespoons' worth of dill. Set aside.

4 Fill the stockpot half full of water. Cut 1 of the lemons into thin, round slices and place in the pot. Add 1 tablespoon salt and 1 tablespoon whole peppercorns. Put the pot over medium heat on the back burner of the stove. Put it on the back burner literally—not figuratively. It's a high-priority pot of water— it will be for the lobster.

5 Rinse the asparagus, then cut off and discard the butts (the bottom 1" to 2"). Set aside the spears. Peel the garlic and discard the paper husks. Finely dice and set aside.

6 Slice the baguette and place the slices in a mixing bowl. Set the bowl on the table.

7 Cut the remaining lemon into 4 quarters. Place 2 wedges on each of the dinner plates. These are for squeezing over the lobster.

In progress: Wine chilling, potatoes baking, lobster water heating, asparagus waiting

Time remaining: 25 to 30 minutes

Things left to do: Sauté mushrooms, boil lobster, finish potatoes, boil asparagus

Get
Cooking

1 Make the mushrooms: Pour 2 tablespoons oil into the large frying pan and put it on the stove over medium heat. When the oil is hot (when it looks runny), add the garlic and cook for 1 minute. Add the mushrooms and cook for 3 to 4 minutes, stirring frequently, until mushrooms begin to soften. Stir in ½ cup white wine. Reduce the heat to low and cook for another 5 minutes. Add the chopped parsley. Lightly salt and grind on pepper. Remove from the heat and toss. Pour into the other mixing bowl and cover with foil to keep warm.

2 Fill the medium saucepan half full of water and put it on the stove over medium-high heat. This will be for the asparagus. Give the potatoes a quick stir.

3 The stockpot of water should be boiling by now. Add the lobster tails and boil for 7 to 8 minutes. Set the timer.

4 Check on the potatoes: After they have been cooking for 30 to 40 minutes, poke them with a knife to make sure they're soft all the way through. Assuming they are, remove them from the oven. Add the chopped dill and toss. Cover with foil and set on the stovetop to keep warm.

5 When the saucepan of water is boiling, add the asparagus and cook for 3 to 4 minutes, or until bright green and tender. Pour the asparagus into the strainer to drain. Put it back in the pan, drizzle with oil, and salt and grind on pepper to taste. Put on the dinner plates.

6 Wash the saucepan, put it back on the burner, and reduce the heat to low. Add 1 stick of butter to melt for the lobster.

7 When the timer goes off, the lobster should be done. Pour it into the strainer to drain it. Use the scissors to carefully cut down the middle of each lobster shell without damaging the meat. Peel off and discard the shells. Turn off the oven and any burners. Arrange the lobster tails and potatoes on the dinner plates so they look good. Pour the melted butter into 2 cereal bowls. Serve.

The extreme steam and multitasking are behind you. Celebrate and dig in.

The mushrooms are to be eaten on the bread, as a starter. When you feel you're in control of the cooking process, don't be afraid to start in on these.

Drink This

Lindemans Bin 65 Chardonnay, <$10

Beringer Founders' Estate Chardonnay, <$15

Louis Latour Mâcon-Lugny, <$15

Play This

Air, *Moon Safari*

Thelonious Monk, *Thelonious Alone in San Francisco*

The Pernice Brothers, *Overcome by Happiness*

What It Really Is:
Shrimp Tacos, Rice, Beans, and Zucchini

What You Tell Her It Is:
Pan-Seared Cilantro Prawns with Saffron Rice & Salsa, Accompanied by Spicy Black Beans, Sautéed Zucchini, & Warm Tortillas

**Cooking time, from prep to plate:
approximately 90 minutes**

Mucho

Here's a mucho Mexicali shrimp surprise with more spice and hot, pink flesh than Cinemax. Put your cooking to the citrus litmus test and make these decapitated decapods dance the salsa! *Es mucho macho.*

Ingredients to Buy

5	lemons
2	bunches fresh cilantro
1	bottle Chef Paul Prudhomme's Seafood Magic
1¼	pounds peeled, deveined jumbo shrimp
2	small yellow onions
1	small red onion
2	small zucchini
4	Roma (plum) tomatoes
1	lime
1	half bottle (375 milliliters) white wine (get a cheapie)
1	package Spanish saffron
1	box white rice
1	can (15 ounces) black beans
1	bottle red pepper flakes
1	package (12) 6" soft corn tortillas

SHOPPING TIP: Look for Chef Paul Prudhomme's Seafood Magic in the dry-spice section of your supermarket. Note Chef Prudhomme's uncanny resemblance to a certain *Cannonball Run* star.

DID YOU KNOW? Saffron comes from a small purple crocus flower. Each crocus contains 3 stigmas, which must be harvested by hand. It takes nearly 5,000 flowers to yield a single ounce of saffron. No wonder it's the priciest spice on earth.

Buy long-grain rice. It's similar to short-grain rice except the grain is longer.

Ingredients You Should Already Have

4 cloves garlic
1 box kosher salt
1 teaspoon fresh ground + millful black peppercorns
1 bottle extra virgin olive oil

Kitchen Equipment

Strainer   2 mixing bowls   Cutting board   Chef's and/or paring knives   Whisk   Plastic wrap
Medium saucepan with lid   Timer   Small saucepan   Aluminum foil   Large frying pan
Small baking pan   4 dinner plates

David Copperfield made this recipe at home. By the time he'd added Chef Prudhomme's magic powder, his marinade had mysteriously vanished. It later turned up in his sock drawer.

1 If you will be drinking white wine, put it in the fridge.

2 Make the marinade for the shrimp: Set the strainer in a mixing bowl. Cut 4 of the lemons in half and, holding them above the strainer, squeeze the juice out of them. Discard the rinds, seeds, and pulp. Rinse the cilantro, shake it dry, and cut off and discard the stems. Finely chop the leaves and add half of them to the bowl. Set aside the other half. Peel the garlic and discard the paper husks. Finely dice the garlic and add to the bowl. Add 3 tablespoons Chef Paul Prudhomme's Seafood Magic, 1 tablespoon salt, and 1 teaspoon pepper. Whisk in ¾ cup oil. Add the shrimp. Toss to coat evenly. Put the bowl in the fridge. Shrimp will need to soak for at least an hour. Note the time and continue with steps 3 through 4.

3 Cut off the tops of the yellow onions, then peel off and discard the skins. Finely dice the onions and set them aside. Repeat with the red onion.

4 Rinse the zucchini. Cut off and discard the ends. Slice the zukes into ¼" disks.

5 Make the salsa: Rinse the tomatoes and cut them in half. Scoop out and discard the seeds. Dice the tomatoes and put them in the other mixing bowl. Add ¼ cup of the red onion and ¼ cup of the cilantro. Set the strainer back in the bowl. Cut the lime and the remaining lemon in half. Hold 1 lemon half and 1 lime half above the strainer and squeeze the juice out of them. Discard the rinds, seeds, and pulp. Lightly salt the salsa and mix thoroughly. Taste to make sure it is salted to your liking. Cover the bowl with plastic wrap and put it in the fridge.

6 Cut the remaining lemon and lime halves into quarters and set aside.

When the shrimp has soaked for an hour, continue with "Get Cooking" step 1.

In progress: Wine chilling, shrimp soaking, zucchini waiting, salsa chilling
Time remaining: 25 to 30 minutes
Things left to do: Cook rice, cook beans, warm tortillas, fry shrimp, cook zucchini

Get Cooking

1 Set the oven to 300°F.

2 Get started on the rice: Pour 2 tablespoons oil into the medium saucepan and put it on the stove over medium heat. When the oil is hot (when it looks runny), add half of the diced yellow onions. Cook, stirring, until soft (2 to 3 minutes). Add ¼ cup white wine and 3 pinches of saffron threads. Cook until the liquid has mostly evaporated (3 to 4 minutes). Add 1 cup rice and 2 cups water. Cook, following the directions on the rice package. The rice should take 20 minutes. Continue with step 3 but set the timer so you don't forget about the rice. When the rice is done, remove it from the heat, leaving the pan covered.

3 Cook the beans: Pour 2 tablespoons oil into the small saucepan and put it on the stove over medium heat. Add the remaining yellow onions and cook until soft. Add the black beans, half of the remaining cilantro, and 2 teaspoons red pepper flakes. Lightly salt. Reduce the heat to low and cook, stirring occasionally, until you're ready to serve the meal.

4 Wrap the tortillas in foil and place them in the oven.

5 Cook the shrimp: Pour 2 tablespoons oil into the large frying pan and put it on the stove over high heat. When the oil is hot, add the shrimp. Cook for 2 minutes on each side, or until opaque. Pour the shrimp and any liquid from the frying pan into the small baking pan. Put the baking pan in the oven to keep warm. Wash the frying pan; you'll need it again in the next step, for the zucchini.

Drink This

Joh. Jos. Prüm Riesling
Kabinett, <$10

Pierre Sparr Gewürztraminer
Carte d'Or, <$15

Beer of your choice

Play This

Mazzy Star, *So Tonight That I
Might See*

Charles Mingus, *Mingus Ah Um*

Willie Nelson,
Red Headed Stranger

6 Cook the zucchini: Add 2 tablespoons oil to the frying pan you used to cook the shrimp and put it on the stove over medium-high heat. When the oil is hot, add the zucchini and cook for 3 to 5 minutes, until slightly golden. Lightly salt and grind on pepper. Turn off all the burners.

7 Fluff the rice with a fork. Place a scoop of rice on each of 2 dinner plates. Spoon the beans and zucchini around the rice. Pull the shrimp out of the oven and arrange it in a pinwheel formation around the rice. Don't forget to turn off the oven. Lightly sprinkle with the remaining cilantro. Get the salsa out of the fridge and put a scoop on each scoop of rice. Place the lemon and lime wedges on the plates as a garnish. Remove the tortillas from the oven, take them out of the foil, place them on the third dinner plate, and cover with the fourth dinner plate to keep warm. Serve.

Good going, guy. When you're done eating, wait at least an hour before you go swimming.

What It Really Is:

Sole, Mini-Broccoli, Rice, and Toast

What You Tell Her It Is:

Pan-Seared Sole in a Lemon Beurre Blanc Sauce, with Blanched Broccolini, Rice Pilaf, & Tomato-Basil Crostini

Cooking time, from prep to plate:
approximately 75 minutes

Saucy

If you're looking for a SWF, you'll find it in this super white fish. The mere notion of sole for two may seem to be a paradox, but this dish is actually a paradigm of paradise. Serve it with a couple of things ending in *ini* and . . . voilà! Good things happen to those who make this. Time to get saucy!

Ingredients to Buy

2	lemons
1	shallot
1	bunch fresh parsley
1	jar water-packed capers
6	Roma (plum) tomatoes
1	bunch fresh basil
1	half bottle (375 milliliters) white wine (get a cheapie)
1	can (14½ ounces) chicken broth
1	box rice pilaf
1	French baguette
1	small bag all-purpose flour
2	sole fillets (½ pound each)
1	bunch Broccolini

Capers are the same size that you would imagine chicken testicles to be. They're just tastier than you would imagine chicken testicles to be.

Ingredients You Should Already Have

2 sticks salted butter
2 cloves garlic
1 bottle extra virgin olive oil
1 box kosher salt
1 bottle finely ground white pepper

Sole, contrary to its name, is not a funky fish. At least not when it's fresh. **DID YOU KNOW?** Because of its flat, elongated shape, sole was called *solea Jovi*—or Jupiter's sandal—by the ancient Romans.

The name Broccolini commands serious respect. Just keep it on the other side of the cutting board from the Crostini family.

Kitchen Equipment

Strainer   3 mixing bowls   Cutting board   Chef's and/or paring knives   3 small plates
2 large frying pans   Whisk   Small saucepan   Medium saucepan   Bread knife   Baking sheet
2 dinner plates

1 Set the oven to 350°F. If you will be drinking white wine, put it in the fridge.

2 Set the strainer in a mixing bowl. Cut the lemons in half and, holding them above the strainer, squeeze the juice out of them. Discard the rinds, seeds, and pulp. Set aside the bowl of juice.

3 Cut off the top of the shallot. Peel off and discard the skin. Finely dice the shallot and set it aside. Rinse a handful of parsley, shake it dry, and cut off the stems. Coarsely chop the leaves and set them aside. Roughly chop 2 table-spoons capers. Set aside.

4 Put 1 stick of butter on a small plate and slice it into eight 1-tablespoon squares (tablespoon measurements are indicated on the butter wrapper). Put it in the fridge.

5 Make the topping for the toast: Rinse the tomatoes and cut them in half. Scoop out and discard the seeds. Finely dice the tomatoes and put them in a second mixing bowl. Peel the garlic and discard the paper husks. Cut the garlic into very thin slices and add to the tomatoes. Stack 8 basil leaves and roll lengthwise (like you would roll, ahem, a cigarette). Cut the roll crosswise into thin slices. Add to the bowl and mix thoroughly. Add a couple of splashes of oil. Salt and pepper to taste. Put the bowl in the fridge.

6 Get started on the sauce for the fish: Put a large frying pan on the stove over medium-high heat. Get the butter out of the fridge, add 1 square to the pan, and let it melt. Add the shallot and cook, stirring, until it becomes soft. Add the lemon juice, the capers, and ½ cup white wine. Cook until ¾ of the liquid has evaporated. This will take about 10 minutes.

"First you hydrate. Then you evaporate. In order to concentrate." —Abraham Lincoln's Gettysburg Address (first draft)

**What heats up
must cook down.**

7 Add 1 cup chicken broth and cook until half of the total liquid has evaporated. This will take about 10 minutes. Reduce the heat to low and whisk in the 7 remaining squares of butter, one at a time, until the sauce becomes creamy. Lightly salt and pepper. Remove from the heat.

In progress: Wine chilling, toast topping chilling, fish sauce waiting
Time remaining: 25 to 30 minutes
Things left to do: Cook rice pilaf, make crostini, fry fish, boil Broccolini

Get Cooking

1 Make the rice pilaf: In the small saucepan, cook it according to the directions on the box.

2 Fill the medium saucepan half full of water and put it on the stove over medium-high heat. This will be for the Broccolini.

3 Make the toast: Slice the baguette into ½"-wide disks and lay them flat on the baking sheet. Drizzle with oil. Lightly salt and pepper. Put the pan on the top shelf in the oven and bake until the bread is lightly toasted (8 to 10 minutes).

4 Get started on the fish: In the remaining mixing bowl, combine ½ cup flour, 1 tablespoon salt, and 1 tablespoon pepper. Mix thoroughly. Add the fish fillets one at a time, flipping each to evenly coat both sides. Set aside.

5 Cook the fish: Put the other large frying pan on the stove over medium heat and melt ¼ of the remaining stick of butter (2 tablespoons). Add the fish fillets in a single layer and cook until the outside is golden brown and the inside is white all the way through (about 2 minutes each side). While the fish is cooking, rewarm the pan of fish sauce over low heat. (Make sure it doesn't boil.)

6 Cook the Broccolini: By now, the saucepan of water should be boiling. Add the Broccolini and cook until it turns bright green (2 to 3 minutes). Pour into the strainer to drain. Turn off the burner. Drizzle the Broccolini with oil, then salt and pepper to taste.

7 Arrange the fish, pilaf, and Broccolini on the dinner plates. Spoon the fish sauce over the fillets and sprinkle lightly with chopped parsley. Spoon the tomato topping on the toast disks and arrange them on the 2 clean small plates. Turn off the oven and any burners. Serve.

Nice work. Slap yourself a high five and get eating.

Drink This

Beringer Founders' Estate
Chardonnay, <$15

Louis Jadot
Mâcon-Villages, <$15

Louis Latour
Mâcon-Lugny, <$15

Play This

Chet Baker, *The Best of Chet Baker Sings*

Richard Hawley, *Late Night Final*

Paul Motian, *Paul Motian on Broadway, Vols. 1–3*

What It Really Is:
Swordfish, Veggies, Potatoes, and Toast

What You Tell Her It Is:
Mediterranean-Style Baked Swordfish with Roasted Vegetables, Parsleyed Potatoes, & Bruschetta with Chèvre & Roasted Red Peppers

Cooking time, from prep to plate:
approximately 60 minutes

Frenzy

Provoke a feeding frenzy with your chum! Of all the fish in the sea, swordfish is definitely one of them. This repast finds said fish collaborating with its old pal lemon as well as making new friends along the way. Don't wait, hesitate, vacillate, or vegetate; it's time to fish or cut bait.

Ingredients to Buy

2	swordfish steaks (³/₄ pound each)
2	lemons
12-15	baby red potatoes
1	medium zucchini
1	red bell pepper
1	yellow bell pepper
1	medium yellow onion
1	can (14 ounces) diced tomatoes
1	bunch fresh parsley
1	small French baguette
1	jar roasted red peppers
1	small log goat cheese (chèvre)

Ingredients You Should Already Have

4 cloves garlic
1 bottle extra virgin olive oil
1 box kosher salt
1 bottle finely ground white pepper
1 stick salted butter

DID YOU KNOW? Swordfish can grow to weigh over 1,000 pounds.

Baby red potatoes are a little larger than the crab apples you used to throw at that dorky kid on your block.

Goat cheese is made from the milk of:
> (a) a yak
> (b) an ape-man
> (c) a nostril
> (d) none of the above

Kitchen Equipment

Large baking pan   Strainer   Medium saucepan with lid   Cutting board   Chef's and/or paring knives
Bread knife   Baking sheet   Timer   Aluminum foil   2 small plates   2 dinner plates

Many years ago, a Polish scientist set out to create an oven with a setting of HALF-BAKE. He really hadn't thought the whole thing through.

1 Set the oven to 375°F. If you will be drinking white wine, put it in the fridge.

2 Start prepping the fish: Rinse it in cold water, pat it dry with paper towels, and place it in the large baking pan. Cut 1 of the lemons in half and, holding the halves over the strainer, squeeze the juice over the fish. Discard the lemon rinds, seeds, and pulp. Set aside the pan. Wash the strainer; you'll need to use it again, for the diced tomatoes.

3 Scrub the potatoes under cold running water. Scrub gently; you're trying to clean the spuds, not exfoliate them. Set them aside. Fill the medium saucepan half full of water and put it on the stove over medium-high heat. This will be for the potatoes.

4 Rinse the zucchini and bell peppers. Cut off and discard the ends of the zucchini. Cut the zuke into ¼"-thick disks. Cut the peppers in half; re-move and discard the stems and seeds. Slice the peppers into ¼"-wide strips. Peel the garlic and discard the paper husks. Finely dice the garlic. Cut off and discard the top of the onion. Peel off and discard the skin. Slice the onion into ½" circular cross sections (like you would put on hamburgers). Over the sink, pour the diced tomatoes into the strainer to drain them.

5 Continue prepping the fish: Arrange the zucchini, pepper strips, and tomatoes around (not on) the fish. Sprinkle with the chopped garlic. Drizzle with oil. Separate the onion slices into rings and lay them over the fish and veggies. Lightly salt and pepper.

6 Rinse a handful of parsley and shake it dry. Cut off and discard the stems, then coarsely chop the leaves. Set aside.

7 Start prepping the toast: Slice the baguette into ½"-wide discs and lay them flat on the baking sheet. Lightly drizzle with oil. Set aside.

8 Drain the liquid from the roasted peppers. Slice the peppers into ¼"-thick strips. Set aside.

You've had a hard week. Have your intern finish the recipe from here.

In progress: Wine chilling, potato water heating, fish and veggies mingling, bread waiting

Time remaining: 25 to 35 minutes

Things left to do: Bake fish and veggies, boil potatoes, toast bread

1 Get the fish and veggies cooking: Place the pan on the lowest oven rack. Everything will have to bake for 25 to 30 minutes. Set the timer.

2 Boil the potatoes: By now, the saucepan of water should be boiling. Add the taters. Boil for 15 to 17 minutes, or until they're soft all the way through when you stab them with a knife. Pour into the strainer to drain. Put back in the warm saucepan and reduce the heat to low. Add ½ stick of butter and a handful of the chopped parsley. Stir until the potatoes are evenly covered with butter and parsley. Cover the pan and turn off the burner.

3 Check on the fish: When the timer goes off, see whether the fish is opaque white and firm to the touch. If not, return it to the oven for another 3 to 5 minutes. When it's done, remove the pan from the oven and cover with foil.

4 Finish the toast: Place the sheet of bread on the top oven rack. Bake for 7 to 10 minutes. When the bread is lightly toasted, remove it from the oven. Don't forget to turn off the oven. Evenly spread the goat cheese on the toast and top with the roasted peppers. Salt and pepper to taste. Put a piece of toast on each of the small plates and set them on the table.

5 Divide the fish, vegetables, and potatoes between the dinner plates. Spoon the juice from the large baking pan over the fish and veggies. Put a thin slice of butter on each piece of fish. Sprinkle with the remaining chopped parsley. Cut the remaining lemon into wedges and put 1 on each plate for squeezing over the fish.

Touché!

Drink This

Lindemans Bin 65 **Chardonnay,** <$10

Bonny Doon **Big House Red,** <$15

Piero Antinori **Chianti Classico,** $15+

Play This

Peter Bruntnell, *Normal for Bridgwater*

John Cale, *Paris 1919*

The Zombies, *Odyssey and Oracle*

No Meat

What It Really Is:
Tomato-Basil Pasta, Salad, and Toast

What You Tell Her It Is:
Linguine with Tomato Concassé & Basil Chiffonade, Caesar Salad, & Pesto-Parmesan Crostini

Cooking time, from prep to plate: approximately 60 minutes

Rustic

Fill her up—with the meal that spawned the term *stuff your face*. From the folks who love combining garlic with more garlic comes this neoclassical Roman aroma-rama. These rustic, old-world noodles proclaim that tomato goes with basil like Simon goes with Garfunkel. Cook this and be more significant to your other.

Ingredients to Buy

2	lemons
1	bottle Worcestershire sauce
½	pound block Parmesan cheese
10	Roma (plum) tomatoes
1	bunch fresh basil
1	small head radicchio
1	package romaine hearts
1	small box grape tomatoes
1	package croutons
1	French baguette
1	container (8 ounces) prepared pesto
1	package fresh linguine

November 12, 1847: Worcestershire sauce is so named when an English gentleman tastes the concoction and asks, "What's this here sauce?"

SHOPPING TIP: A head of radicchio is about the size of a grapefruit. It has dark red leaves with prominent white veins and is found near the lettuce.

DID YOU KNOW? The Italian word *linguine* literally means "little tongues."

Ingredients You Should Already Have

5 cloves garlic

1 bottle red wine vinegar

1 jar Dijon mustard

1 bottle extra virgin olive oil

1 box kosher salt

Millful black peppercorns

Olive oil = food lubricant

Kitchen Equipment

Strainer   3 mixing bowls   Cutting board   Chef's and/or paring knives   Whisk   Vegetable peeler
Grater   Salad bowl   Plastic wrap   Stockpot   Bread knife   Baking sheet   3 dinner plates
2 small plates

Please turn off all cell phones and beepers at this time.

1 Set the oven to 350°F.

2 Make the salad dressing: Set the strainer in a mixing bowl. Cut the lemons in half and, holding them above the strainer, squeeze the juice out of them. Discard the rinds, seeds, and pulp. Peel 2 of the garlic cloves and discard the paper husks. Chop the garlic as finely as possible and add to the bowl. Add ¼ cup red wine vinegar, 2 tablespoons mustard, and 2 splashes of Worcestershire sauce. Mix thoroughly. Whisk in ½ cup oil. Salt and grind in pepper to taste. Set aside. All hail Caesar!

3 With the vegetable peeler, shave half of the Parmesan block into paper-thin strips. Set aside. With the grater, finely grate the remainder of the cheese into a second mixing bowl. Set aside.

4 Make the pasta sauce: Rinse the Roma tomatoes and cut them into quarters. Scoop out and discard the seeds. Finely chop the tomatoes and put them into the third mixing bowl. Stack 6 large basil leaves and roll them lengthwise (like you would roll a cigarette). Cut the roll crosswise into thin slices and add them to the bowl. Repeat with another 6 basil leaves. Peel the remaining 3 garlic cloves and discard the paper husks. Finely chop and add to the bowl. Add ½ cup oil and mix thoroughly. Salt and grind on pepper to taste. Set aside.

5 Make the salad: Peel off and discard the outermost leaves of the radicchio. Cut off the butt ends of the radicchio and 2 romaine hearts. Chop all the leaves crosswise into ½"-wide pieces and put them in the salad bowl. Rinse the grape tomatoes, slice them in half lengthwise, and add them to the bowl. Sprinkle a handful of croutons over the salad and top with half of the shaved Parmesan. Cover the bowl with plastic wrap and put it in the fridge.

In progress: Pasta sauce chilling, salad chilling
Time remaining: 15 to 20 minutes
Things left to do: Make toast, dress salad, boil linguine

Get Cooking

1 Fill the stockpot half full of water and put it on the stove over high heat. Add 1 tablespoon oil and 1 tablespoon salt. This will be for the linguine.

2 Make the toast: Slice the baguette into ½"-wide disks and lay them flat on the baking sheet. Spread each disk with pesto and sprinkle with the grated Parmesan. Put the pan on the middle oven rack and bake until the cheese is golden brown (8 to 10 minutes). Remove the pan from the oven and arrange the bread on a dinner plate. Turn off the oven. Set the plate on the table.

3 Dress the salad: Get the salad out of the fridge. Whisk the dressing, pour over the salad, and toss. Sprinkle with half of the remaining shaved Parmesan and place on the table with the 2 small plates.

4 By now, the linguine water should be boiling. Reduce the heat to medium-high and cook the linguine according to the directions on the package. Pour it into the strainer to drain and shake off the excess water.

5 Turn off the burner and put the linguine back in the pot. Add 2 tablespoons oil and toss. Serve on the other 2 dinner plates. Top with the pasta sauce. Add the remaining shaved Parmesan and serve.

Great job. Before you sit down, take a moment to stretch your calves. It's been a while since you've done that.

Drink This

Navarro Correas **Malbec, <$15**

Ravenswood **Zinfandel Vintners Blend, <$15**

Piero Antinori **Chianti Classico, $15+**

Play This

Paolo Conte, *The Best of Paolo Conte*

Sam Prekop, *Sam Prekop*

Talk Talk, *The Colour of Spring*

What It Really Is:

Pasta with Veggies, Salad, and Bread

What You Tell Her It Is:

Fusilli with Sautéed Baby Spinach & Portobello Mushrooms, Served with Mesclun Salad & Focaccia

Cooking time, from prep to plate:
approximately 60 minutes

Lip Smacker

This celebration of vegetation and carbohydration is the stick-to-your-ribs lip smacker that puts the "fun" in *fungus* and doubles as a highly effective vampire deterrent. Just like some Italian guy's grandma used to make. For ages 18 and up. Minimal assembly required.

Ingredients to Buy

1	yellow onion
3	portobello mushrooms
1	box cherry tomatoes
1	bag prewashed mesclun salad mix
¼	pound block Parmesan cheese
1	bag prewashed baby spinach
1	box fusilli (dry pasta spirals)
1	focaccia (flat Italian bread loaf)
1	half bottle (375 milliliters) white wine (get a cheapie)
1	package (8 ounces) pine nuts

If you don't know what a portobello is, ask the old lady with purple hair who just rammed her cart into your Achilles.

If the only spinach you can find is unwashed rather than prewashed, make sure you rinse it really well. Sandy spinach is about as pleasant as a sandy bathing suit.

DID YOU KNOW? Pine nuts come primarily from the cones of two different conifers, the stone pine and the Chinese pine. Do you care?

Ingredients You Should Already Have

3 cloves garlic
1 box kosher salt
1 bottle extra virgin olive oil
Millful black peppercorns
1 bottle balsamic vinegar
1 stick salted butter

Kitchen Equipment

Cutting board   Chef's and/or paring knives   Salad bowl   Vegetable peeler   Plastic wrap   Grater
2 mixing bowls   Stockpot with lid   Large frying pan with lid   Bread knife   Baking sheet
3 small plates   Strainer   2 dinner plates

1 Cut off the top of the onion. Peel off and discard the skin. Slice the onion into circular cross sections (like you would put on hamburgers). Cut the cross sections in half. Set aside. Peel the garlic and discard the paper husks. Finely dice the garlic. Set aside.

2 With a paper towel, brush any dirt off the mushrooms. Cut off and discard the dirty parts at the bottoms of the stems. Cut the portobellos into ½" cubes. Set aside.

3 Rinse the tomatoes and pat them dry with paper towels. Cut them into halves and set them aside.

4 Get started on the salad: Open the bag of mesclun and dump the greens into the salad bowl. Add half of the tomatoes.

5 With the vegetable peeler, shave half of the Parmesan block into paper-thin strips. Add the shavings to the salad. Cover the bowl with plastic wrap and put it in the fridge. With the grater, finely grate the remainder of the cheese into a mixing bowl. Set aside. This will be for the pasta and salad.

Crack your knuckles and be thankful you're not wearing a hair net.

In progress: Salad chilling
Time remaining: 25 to 30 minutes
Things left to do: Make pasta topping, boil pasta, warm bread, dress salad

Get Cooking

1 Set the oven to 350°F.

2 Fill the stockpot half full of water. Add 1 tablespoon salt and 1 tablespoon oil. Cover and put the pot on the stove over high heat. This will be for the pasta.

3 Start making the topping for the pasta: Pour 2 tablespoons oil into the large frying pan and put it on the stove over medium-high heat. When the oil is hot (when it looks runny), add the onion and garlic. Cook, stirring frequently, until the onion softens (about 2 minutes). Add the portobellos and cook until soft (about 3 minutes). Add the spinach and cook, stirring, until wilted (about 3 more minutes).

4 By now, the pasta water should be boiling. Reduce the heat to medium-high and cook 2 servings of pasta according to the directions on the box.

5 Warm the bread: Slice it, place it on the baking sheet, and bake for 5 to 8 minutes.

6 Finish the topping for the pasta: Add ¼ cup wine and the remaining tomatoes to the frying pan and cook, stirring, for 1 minute. Lightly salt and grind on pepper. Put the lid on the pan and turn off the burner.

7 Dress the salad: Get it out of the fridge and drizzle with oil and vinegar. Lightly salt and grind on pepper. Toss. Set on the table with 2 of the small plates.

8 When the pasta is done, pour it into the strainer to drain. Turn off the burner, put the pasta back in the pot, and toss in the topping. Mix. Serve on the dinner plates. Lightly sprinkle with the pine nuts and grated Parmesan. Place the warmed bread in the other mixing bowl and set it on the table. Turn off the oven. Place the butter on the third small plate and set it on the table, too.

Pat yourself on the back. Serve up and chow down.

Drink This

Taurino Salice Salentino Riserva, <$10

Argiolas Costera, <$15

Piero Antinori Chianti Classico, $15+

Play This

Miles Davis, *Porgy and Bess*

Ronnie Lane and Slim Chance, *Anymore for Anymore*

Tom Waits, *Closing Time*

What It Really Is:
Pasta and Mushrooms, with Salad and Bread

What You Tell Her It Is:
Farfalle and Mixed Wild Mushrooms, with Insalata Caprese & Focaccia

Cooking time, from prep to plate:
approximately 60 minutes

Caboodle

Get rich quick! These semiformal pasta bow ties are all dressed up with nowhere to go but down the hatch. As surely as a European exchange student sports a fanny pack, this entire mushroom-melange kit and noodle caboodle is guaranteed to wow the woman of your fancy. A truly heavenly garden of eatin'.

Ingredients to Buy

4	vine-ripened tomatoes
1	large ball (about ½ pound) fresh mozzarella
1	bunch fresh basil
1	bunch fresh Italian (flat-leaf) parsley
1	pound mixed wild mushrooms
1	bottle red pepper flakes
1	lemon
1	carton (½ pint) heavy cream
1	box farfalle (dry bow tie pasta)
1	focaccia (flat Italian bread loaf)
1	container (8 ounces) freshly grated Parmesan cheese

DID YOU KNOW? Mozzarella accounts for approximately 30 percent of the total amount of cheese produced in the United States each year.

SHOPPING TIP: If you can't find mixed wild mushrooms per se, buy 1 large portobello, ¼ pound shiitakes, and ¼ pound creminis.

Ingredients You Should Already Have

1 bottle extra virgin olive oil
1 bottle balsamic vinegar
1 tablespoon + shakerful kosher salt
Millful black peppercorns
2 cloves garlic
1 stick salted butter

Kitchen Equipment

Cutting board   Chef's and/or paring knives   3 small plates   Plastic wrap   Stockpot
Large frying pan   Strainer   Baking sheet   Bread knife   2 dinner plates   Mixing bowl

Somebody needs to invent a microwave that makes things cold fast.

1 If you will be drinking white wine, put it in the fridge.

2 Make the salad: Rinse the tomatoes, then cut out and discard the stem portions. Slice the tomatoes into thin, circular cross sections (like you would put on hamburgers). Cut the mozzarella into slices of the same thickness as the tomatoes. Stack 6 large leaves basil and roll them lengthwise (like you would roll a cigarette). Cut the roll crosswise into thin slices. Repeat with another 6 leaves. Lay the tomato slices on 2 of the small plates. Lay the mozzarella slices on the tomatoes and drizzle with oil and vinegar. Lightly salt and grind on pepper. Top with the chopped basil. Cover the salads with plastic wrap and put them in the fridge.

3 Peel the garlic and discard the paper husks. Finely dice the garlic and set aside. Rinse a handful of parsley and shake dry. Cut off and discard the stems. Finely chop the leaves. Set aside. With a paper towel, brush any dirt off the mushrooms. Chop coarsely. To properly chop coarsely, put on a white, malt liquor–stained tank top. Next, light a cigarette on the stovetop and cuss liberally. Commence chopping. When finished, set aside the mushrooms.

4 Fill the stockpot half full of water and put it on the stove over high heat. Add 1 tablespoon oil and 1 tablespoon salt. This will be for the pasta.

In progress: Wine chilling, salad chilling, pasta water heating
Time remaining: 30 minutes
Things left to do: Make pasta sauce, boil pasta, warm bread

Get
Cooking

1 Set the oven to 350°F.

2 Make the pasta sauce: Pour 3 tablespoons oil into the large frying pan and put the pan on the stove over high heat. When the oil is hot (when it looks runny), add the mushrooms and cook for 1 to 2 minutes, stirring frequently. Add the garlic and cook for 3 to 4 minutes, stirring frequently. Add 1 teaspoon red pepper flakes. Cut the lemon in half and, holding 1 of the halves over the strainer, squeeze the juice over the pan. Discard the rind, seeds, and pulp. Cook the sauce until the juice has evaporated. This will take 1 to 2 minutes. Reduce the heat to medium. Add the cream and cook until half of the liquid has evaporated. This will take another 6 to 8 minutes. Lightly salt and grind on pepper. Stir the sauce. Turn off the burner. Wash the strainer; you'll need to use it again, for the pasta.

3 By now, the pasta water should be boiling. Reduce the heat to medium-high and cook 2 servings of pasta according to the directions on the box.

4 Warm the bread: Slice it, place it on the baking sheet, and bake for 5 to 8 minutes.

5 When the pasta is done, pour it into the strainer to drain and shake off excess water. Turn off the burner and put the pasta back in the pot. Add ½ cup Parmesan, ½ stick of butter, 2 tablespoons parsley, and 1 tablespoon oil. Toss. Add the mushroom sauce and toss.

6 Serve the pasta on the dinner plates and lightly sprinkle with the remaining parsley and Parmesan. Remove the salads from the fridge and serve. Place the warmed bread in the mixing bowl and set it on the table. Turn off the oven. Pour some oil on the third small plate and set it on the table as a lube for the bread.

Mangiamo! (Rough translation: "Get your punk ass to the table.")

Drink This

Beringer Founders' Estate
Chardonnay, <$15

Louis Jadot
Mâcon-Villages, <$15

Louis Latour
Mâcon-Lugny, <$15

Play This

Bee Gees, *Best of Bee Gees*

Neil Halstead,
Sleeping on Roads

Massive Attack, *Blue Lines*

What It Really Is:
Ravioli, Asparagus, and Bread

What You Tell Her It Is:
Cheese-Spinach Ravioli in Butter Sauce, with Chilled Balsamic Asparagus Salad & Garlic Bread

Cooking time, from prep to plate:
approximately 60 minutes

Cheesier

Dairy chic! Our runway sources in Paris have confirmed that butter and cheese are back in fashion this season. Richer than the Sultan of Brunei, cheesier than your old acid-washed jeans, and more decadent than any given night with Van Halen circa 1980, this savory spread combines such sideshow oddities as chilled spears and shaved cheese.

Ingredients to Buy

1	shallot
1	bunch fresh sage
¼	pound block Parmesan cheese
1	French baguette
1	container garlic powder
1	bunch asparagus
1	pound fresh cheese-spinach ravioli

A shallot is kind of like an onion with a Napoleon complex.

When buying a baguette, resist the temptation to reenact the lightsaber scene from *Star Wars*. It'll take more than bread to beat the Dark Side.

SHOPPING TIP: Fresh ravioli will be in the refrigerator aisle of your grocery store.

Ingredients You Should Already Have

1 bottle extra virgin olive oil
1 box kosher salt
1 stick salted butter
Millful black peppercorns
1 bottle balsamic vinegar

Kitchen Equipment

Cutting board   Chef's and/or paring knives   Vegetable peeler   Grater   Mixing bowl
Medium saucepan with lid   Bread knife   Baking sheet   Strainer   Large frying pan   2 small plates
Plastic wrap

Get Started (Rinsing, Mincing,

Slicing, & Dicing)

1 Set the oven to 350°F. If you will be drinking white wine, put it in the fridge.

2 Cut off the top of the shallot. Peel off and discard the skin. Finely dice the shallot. Set aside.

3 Stack 6 sage leaves and roll them lengthwise (like you would roll a cigarette). Cut the roll crosswise into thin slices. Repeat with another 6 leaves. Set aside. Do not attempt to smoke sage.

4 With the vegetable peeler, shave half of the Parmesan block into paper-thin strips. Set aside. Finely grate the remainder into the mixing bowl. Set it aside.

5 Fill the medium saucepan half full of water and put it on the stove over medium-high heat. This will be for the asparagus.

6 Get started making the bread: Slice the baguette lengthwise and separate it into 2 halves. Put the halves on the baking sheet, cut side up. Lightly drizzle with oil. Sprinkle with garlic powder and half of the grated Parmesan. Set aside.

7 Cook the asparagus: Rinse it, then cut off and discard the butts (the bottom 1" to 2"). When the pan of water is boiling, add the asparagus. Cook for 3 to 4 minutes, until bright green and tender. Pour it into the strainer to drain and set aside to cool.

You have a few loose ends dangling here. Prepare to undangle them.

In progress: Wine chilling, bread waiting, asparagus cooling
Time remaining: 20 minutes
Things left to do: Make pasta sauce, make salad, toast bread, boil pasta

1 Refill the medium saucepan half full of water. Add 1 tablespoon oil and 1 tablespoon salt. Cover and put the pan on the stove over high heat. This will be for the ravioli.

2 Make the pasta sauce: Put the large frying pan on the stove over medium-high heat and melt the butter. Add ¼ cup oil and the shallot and cook, stirring, until the shallot softens. Stir in the sage. Lightly salt and grind on pepper. Turn off the burner.

3 Make the salad: On the small plates, arrange the asparagus spears next to each other. Drizzle with oil and vinegar. Sprinkle with the shaved Parmesan and lightly salt and grind on pepper. Cover the plates with plastic wrap and put in the fridge.

4 Heat up the garlic bread: Place the baking sheet on the middle oven rack. Bake for 10 to 12 minutes.

5 By now, the ravioli water should be boiling. Reduce the heat to medium-high and cook the ravioli according to the directions on the package. (Fresh ravioli is generally done when it begins floating.) Follow the ravioli-box directions closely. Thinking outside the box may result in ruined pasta.

6 It's time to reheat the sauce: Put the frying pan (with the sauce in it) back on the stove over low heat. Give a quick stir.

7 When the ravioli is done, pour it into the strainer to drain and then arrange it on 2 of the dinner plates. Spoon on the sauce and cover with the remaining grated Parmesan. Lightly salt and grind on pepper. Set the plates on the table.

8 Remove the bread from the oven and slice it. Place it on the third dinner plate and set it on the table. Turn off the oven and any burners. Get the salads out of the fridge and serve.

Nice work. You just made Chef Boyardee look like a chump.

Drink This

Lindemans Bin 65
Chardonnay, <$10

Beringer Founders' Estate
Chardonnay, <$15

Louis Latour
Mâcon-Lugny, <$15

Play This

Nick Drake, *Pink Moon*

Everything but the Girl,
Amplified Heart

Willie Nelson,
Red Headed Stranger

What It Really Is:

Creamy Yellow Rice, Asparagus, Salad, and Bread

What You Tell Her It Is:

Risotto Milanese, with Blanched Asparagus, Salad of Mixed Baby Greens with Mustard Vinaigrette, & Ciabatta

Cooking time, from prep to plate: approximately 60 minutes

Lotto

Good things happen when risotto and saffron party together. Take this gold, plated Italianate dish, for instance. It's a creamy, steamy, and dreamy tour de force that is both saladventuresome and full of asparagusto. Win over that special someone with this, your risotto-lotto meal ticket.

Ingredients to Buy

1	bag prewashed mesclun salad mix
1	small box grape tomatoes
1	bottle Champagne vinegar
1	bunch fresh Italian (flat-leaf) parsley
1	yellow onion
1	bunch asparagus
1	ciabatta (long, wide Italian bread loaf)
¼	pound block Parmesan cheese
1	can (32 ounces) chicken broth
1	box (1 pound) Arborio rice
1	package Spanish saffron
1	half bottle (375 milliliters) white wine (get a cheapie)

Champagne vinegar is what you're left with after someone makes an inappropriate New Year's Eve toast.

DID YOU KNOW? In ancient times, wreaths of parsley were placed on graves to protect the deceased from evil spirits.

Ingredients You Should Already Have

1 clove garlic
1 jar Dijon mustard
1 bottle extra virgin olive oil
1 stick salted butter
1 box kosher salt
Millful black peppercorns

Kitchen Equipment

Salad bowl   Cutting board   Chef's and/or paring knives   Plastic wrap   2 mixing bowls   Whisk
Bread knife   4 small plates   Vegetable peeler   Medium saucepan   Stockpot   Large frying pan
Strainer   2 dinner plates

1 If you will be drinking white wine, put it in the fridge. If you won't be drinking white wine, don't put it in the fridge.

2 Make the salad: Open the bag of mesclun and dump the greens into the salad bowl. Rinse the tomatoes and pat them dry with paper towels. Cut them into halves and sprinkle them over the greens. Cover the bowl with plastic wrap and put it in the fridge.

3 Make the salad dressing: Peel the garlic and discard the paper husk. Finely dice and put in a mixing bowl. Add ¼ cup vinegar and 2 tablespoons mustard. Whisk into a smooth paste. Slowly whisk in ½ cup oil. Set aside the bowl.

4 Rinse a handful of parsley and shake it dry. Cut off and discard the stems. Finely chop the leaves until you have ¼ cup's worth. Set aside. This will be the garnish for your dish.

5 Cut off the top of the onion. Peel off and discard the skin. Finely dice the onion and set it aside. Rinse the asparagus, then cut off and discard the butts (the bottom 1" to 2"). Set aside.

6 Slice the bread, place it in the other mixing bowl, and set the bowl on the table. Put the butter on a small plate and set it on the table, too.

7 With the vegetable peeler, shave half of the Parmesan block into paper-thin strips until you have ½ cup's worth. Set aside.

8 Pour the broth into the medium saucepan and put it on the stove over medium heat.

9 Fill the stockpot half full of water and put it on the stove over medium-high heat. This will be for the asparagus.

In progress: Wine chilling, salad chilling
Time remaining: 25 to 35 minutes
Things left to do: Cook risotto, cook asparagus, dress salad

Get Cooking

1. Cook the risotto: In the large frying pan, combine 1 tablespoon oil and 1 tablespoon butter (tablespoon measurements are indicated on the butter wrapper). Put the pan on the stove over medium-high heat. When the butter is melted, add the onion and cook until it softens (about 2 minutes). Add 1 cup rice and a few pinches of saffron threads. Stir until the rice is evenly coated with oil, butter, and saffron. Add ¾ cup wine and stir until absorbed. Add 1 cup of the hot chicken broth and stir until all the liquid is absorbed. Keep adding broth 1 cup at a time until all of the broth has been incorporated. This will take 15 to 20 minutes. The risotto is done when it is soft to the bite and creamy looking. Finish cooking it before you move on to anything else. Lightly salt and grind on pepper. Turn off the burner.

2. By now, the stockpot of water should be boiling. Add the asparagus and boil for 3 to 4 minutes. Pour it into the strainer to drain.

3. Turn on the burner under the pan of risotto to reheat. Stir. When the risotto is done, mound it on the dinner plates and arrange the asparagus spears on top in pinwheel formation. Top with the shaved Parmesan and chopped parsley. Get the salad out of the fridge. Whisk the dressing, pour over the salad, and toss. Place on the table with the remaining 2 small plates. Turn off all the burners and serve.

You're a true artiste—with an *e*, as in *eat now*.

Drink This

Falesco Est! Est!! Est!!!, <$10

S. Quirico Vernaccia di San Gimignano, <$10

Casa Lapostolle Sauvignon Blanc, <$15

Play This

Serge Gainsbourg, *Couleur Café*

The Jimmy Giuffre 3, *The Jimmy Giuffre 3*

Beth Orton, *Central Reservation*

What It Really Is:

Rice-and-Bean Tacos with Corn

What You Tell Her It Is:

Spanish Rice with Spicy Black Beans, Fire-Roasted Corn, & Fresh Salsa & Guacamole, Served with Warm Tortillas

Cooking time, from prep to plate:
approximately 60 minutes

Mexerciser

Holy mole! Guacamole, that is. A vegetarian meal with some real *cojones*, this spicy, ricey, cilantropic Mexerciser packs more kick than a burro in heat. Cook this if you know what's good for you.

Ingredients to Buy

1   red onion
1   small yellow onion
1   can (14 ounces) fire-roasted diced tomatoes
1   box or bag long-grain white rice
2   bunches fresh cilantro
4   Roma (plum) tomatoes
1   lemon
3   limes
2   avocados
2   ears fresh corn (if you have a gas range)
    or 1 small bag frozen corn kernels
1   package (12) 6" flour tortillas
1   bunch scallions
1   can (14 ounces) black beans
1   bottle red pepper flakes

SHOPPING TIP: If you can't find fire-roasted tomatoes, regular diced tomatoes will suffice.

DID YOU KNOW? The French used to call tomatoes "love apples." No coincidence that Roma backward is Amor.

Avocado: Fruit? Vegetable? Latino lawyer?

Ingredients You Should Already Have

2 cloves garlic
1 stick salted butter
1 box kosher salt
Millful black peppercorns
1 bottle extra virgin olive oil

Kitchen Equipment

Cutting board   Chef's and/or paring knives   Medium saucepan with lid   Strainer   2 mixing bowls   Large 2- or 4-cup liquid measuring cup   Timer   Plastic wrap   Tongs   Aluminum foil   2 large frying pans   4 dinner plates

1 Peel the garlic and discard the paper husks. Finely dice the garlic and set aside. Cut off the tops of the red and yellow onions. Peel off and discard the skins. Finely dice each and set aside.

2 Make the rice: Put 2 tablespoons butter (tablespoon measurements are indicated on the butter wrapper) in the medium saucepan and put the pan on the stove over medium-high heat. When the butter is melted, add ½ cup of the red onion and cook for 2 minutes. Set the strainer in a mixing bowl. Pour the diced tomatoes into the strainer to drain. Pour the tomato juice into the measuring cup and add water until you have 1¼ cups liquid. Add the tomato liquid, diced tomatoes, 1 cup rice, and a pinch of salt to the saucepan. Bring to a boil, then reduce the heat to the lowest setting and cover. The rice will take 20 minutes to cook. Set the timer and continue with step 3. When the timer goes off, remove the rice from the heat, but keep it covered.

3 Make the salsa: Rinse the cilantro and shake dry. Cut off and discard the stems. Finely chop the leaves. Cilantro shortcut: Take the cilantro out back, hose it down, and run over it with the lawn mower. (You didn't hear that from us, by the way.) Rinse the Roma tomatoes and cut them into quarters. Scoop out and discard the seeds. Dice the tomatoes and put them in the mixing bowl in which you drained the diced tomatoes. Add ¼ cup of the red onion and ¼ cup of the cilantro. Set the strainer back in the bowl. Cut the lemon and 1 of the limes in half. Hold 1 lemon half and 1 lime half above the strainer and squeeze the juice out of them. Discard the rinds, seeds, and pulp. Lightly salt the salsa and mix thoroughly. Taste to make sure it is salted to your liking. Cover the bowl with plastic wrap and put it in the fridge.

4 Make the guacamole: Cut the avocados into quarters (like you would cut pears). Remove and discard the pits and skin. Put the avocados in the other mixing bowl and mash with a fork until chunky/creamy. Add $\frac{1}{4}$ cup of the red onion and $\frac{1}{4}$ cup of the cilantro. Set the strainer in the bowl. Hold the remaining lemon half and lime half above the strainer and squeeze the juice out of them. Discard the rinds, seeds, and pulp. Remove the strainer from the bowl and scrape off any guac that stuck to it. Lightly salt the guac and grind on pepper. Mix thoroughly. Taste to make sure it is seasoned to your liking. Cut another of the limes into round slices and place them on top of the guac to keep it from turning brown. Cover the bowl with plastic wrap and put it in the fridge.

5 If your corn is fresh, shuck it. If you're using frozen corn or you don't have a gas range, proceed to "Get Cooking" step 1. If you are cooking with gas (a gas grill will do, too), set one of the burners to high. Use tongs to hold the cobs 1" above the flame and slowly turn them until the kernels are an even roasted-brown color. Turn off the burner and let the cobs cool.

In progress: Rice cooking, salsa chilling, guacamole chilling, corn cooling

Time remaining: 30 minutes

Things left to do: Heat tortillas, cook beans, season the corn

1 Heat the tortillas: Set the oven to 350°F. Wrap the tortillas in foil and place them in the oven.

2 Rinse the scallions and shake them dry. Cut off and discard the roots. Starting from the root end, cut the bottom 5" of each scallion into thin, round slices. Set aside. Cut the kernels off the corn cobs and set aside. (If your corn is frozen, run it under hot water to thaw it, then set it aside.)

3 Make the beans: Over the sink, pour the black beans into the strainer to drain them, then rinse them under cold running water. Pour 2 tablespoons oil into a large frying pan and put it on the stove over medium-high heat. When the oil is hot (when it looks runny), add the yellow onion and the garlic. Cook for 2 to 3 minutes, until the onion softens. Add the beans and 1 teaspoon red pepper flakes. Lightly salt, stir, and reduce the heat to the lowest setting.

4 Put 2 tablespoons butter in the other frying pan and put the pan on the stove over medium-high heat. When the butter is melted, add the corn. Cook for 2 minutes, stirring frequently. Cut the remaining lime in half and squeeze the juice into the pan. Add half of the scallions, stir, and turn off the burner.

5 Add half of the remaining cilantro to the rice and stir.

6 Add the remaining scallions and cilantro to the beans.

7 Divide the rice, beans, and corn between 2 dinner plates. Remove the tortillas from the oven, take them out of the foil, place them on the third dinner plate, and cover with the fourth dinner plate to keep warm. Serve with the salsa and guacamole (remove the lime slices from the guac).

Ay, chihuahua! You just made a lot of food.

Drink This

Beer of your choice

Play This

Peter Bruntnell,
Normal for Bridgwater

Youssou N'Dour,
The Guide (Wommat)

Zero 7, *Simple Things*

Desserts

Desserts

Ahhh. (Burp!) That was great. Great food, great drink, great conversation. And you made it all yourself. (Well, she helped out with the conversation.) Now it's time to kick back, not do the dishes, and try to discreetly unbutton your pants.

Not so fast, Romeo. What about the happy finish? How could you forget the happy finish?! You know—dessert. (What did you think we were talking about?)

We know that after all that shopping and chopping, all that heating, feeding, and eating, the last thing you're going to want to do is engage in anything that could possibly be construed as cooking. That's why we offer six dessert ideas that are easier than pie and versatile enough to chase any meal this side of sweetbreads. Calling these dessert suggestions *recipes* would be a gross overstatement; each one basically entails dumping something sweet on top of something else sweet. They're just that simple.

So if, at the end of your meal, you're not yet ready for your lady friend to desert you, dessert her. After all, she could always eat and run, but it'll be harder for her to eat, eat more, and run. And at the very least, you'll leave her with a good taste in her mouth.

If you want to wash everything down with a mug of java or a snifter of *digestif*, we'll leave you to your own vices. But if you want just desserts, give your sweet talk a rest and give her sweet tooth a workout.

Fresh Strawberries
with Sour Cream & Brown Sugar

This can be made ahead of time.

Ingredients to Buy

1   large carton fresh strawberries
1   container (8 ounces) sour cream
1   small box dark brown sugar

Kitchen Equipment

Mixing bowl
2 cereal bowls

How to Make It

1 Rinse the strawberries and let them drip dry. Put them in the mixing bowl.

2 Spoon the sour cream into a cereal bowl.

3 Dump half of the brown sugar into the other cereal bowl and use a fork to break up the larger chunks.

4 Place all 3 bowls on the table.

How to eat it: Holding a strawberry by the stem, dip it into the sour cream and then the brown sugar.

Lemon Tarts with Fresh Blueberries

This can be made ahead of time.

Ingredients to Buy

2   small lemon tarts (each about 4" wide)

1   carton fresh blueberries

Kitchen Equipment

2 small plates

How to Make It

1 Put each tart on a small plate.

2 Sprinkle a handful of blueberries over each of the tarts.

3 Put the plates in the fridge until you're ready to serve.

Lemon & Berry Sorbet
with Fresh Raspberries

Ingredients to Buy

1   pint lemon sorbet
1   pint strawberry or raspberry sorbet
1   carton fresh raspberries

Kitchen Equipment

2 cereal bowls

How to Make It

1 Put 1 scoop of each sorbet in each of the bowls.

2 Sprinkle a handful of raspberries over the sorbet and serve.

Three Flavors of Japanese Mochi Ice Cream

This can be made ahead of time.

Ingredients to Buy

1   package vanilla mochi ice cream

DID YOU KNOW? Mochi is a Japanese ice cream that comes prepackaged in six 2-ounce portions.

1   package strawberry mochi ice cream

1   package green tea mochi ice cream

Kitchen Equipment

2 cereal bowls

How to Make It

1 Put 1 ball of each flavor of ice cream in each bowl.

2 Put the bowls in the freezer until you're ready to serve them.

Vanilla Bean Ice Cream with Kahlúa, Hot Fudge, Chocolate-Covered Espresso Beans, & Whipped Cream

This requires 5 to 10 minutes to prepare.

Ingredients to Buy

1   can chocolate sauce
1   pint vanilla ice cream
1   small bottle Kahlúa liqueur
1   small bag chocolate-covered espresso beans
1   can whipped cream

Kitchen Equipment

Can opener
Small saucepan
2 cereal bowls

How to Make It

1 Open the can of chocolate sauce, pour the sauce into the small saucepan, and put the pan on the stove over medium-low heat.

2 Put 2 large scoops of ice cream in each bowl.

3 Lightly drizzle the Kahlúa over the ice cream.

4 When the chocolate sauce is warm, liberally pour it over the top of the ice cream.

5 Lightly sprinkle the ice cream with espresso beans.

6 Top the ice cream with a squirt of whipped cream and serve.

Warm Apple Tarts with Vanilla Ice Cream

This requires 15 minutes to prepare.

Ingredients to Buy

2   small apple tarts (each about 4" wide)

1   pint vanilla ice cream

Kitchen Equipment

Baking sheet

2 small plates

How to Make It

1 Set the oven to 350°F.

2 When the oven is hot, place the tarts on the baking sheet and bake for 5 to 10 minutes.

3 Put each tart on a plate and top with a scoop of ice cream. Serve warm.

Aftermath

There you have it. If you've reached this point in the book, you've probably gone the distance and actually cooked at least one meal for a bona fide woman. In the process of so doing, we hope that you've enjoyed yourself—and herself—and that you've discovered an interest in the realm of possibility that lies beyond ramen noodles, Mad Dog, and Hootie.

Most important, we hope things have worked out with what's-her-name. If for some unimaginable reason they haven't, fear not, kitchen comrade: There are plenty of other women out there—and plenty of other recipes in here.

So press PLAY, drink up, and cook on.

Index

Underscored page references indicate marginalia or boxed text. **Boldfaced** references indicate photographs.

A

Adelsheim Pinot Gris, 16, 70, 89
Air, *Moon Safari*, 17, 75, 93
Aluminum foil, 5
Apples
    Steak, Potatoes, Green Beans, and Salad, 29–31
    Warm Apple Tarts with Vanilla Ice Cream, 143
Argentinean wines
    Navarro Correas Malbec, 15, 113
    Trapiche "Oak Cask" Malbec, 14, 35
    Weinert Merlot, 15, 35
Argiolas Costera, 14, 39, 117
Asian-style dishes
    Beef-Asparagus Stir-Fry with Rice and Soybeans, 37–39
    Chicken-and-Veggie Stir-Fry with Rice, 59–61
    Three Flavors of Japanese Mochi Ice Cream, 141
    Tuna, Rice, Veggies, and Cucumber Salad, 83–85
Asparagus
    Beef-Asparagus Stir-Fry with Rice and Soybeans, 37–39
    Creamy Yellow Rice, Asparagus, Salad, and Bread, 127–29
    Lobster, Asparagus, Potatoes, and Bread, 91–93
    Ravioli, Asparagus, and Bread, 123–25
    Tuna, Rice, Veggies, and Cucumber Salad, 83–85
    Veal with Pasta and Asparagus, 41–43
Australian wines
    Lindemans Bin 65 Chardonnay, 16, 93, 108, 125
    Tyrell's Long Flat Red, 14, 52
    Wyndham Estates Bin 555 Shiraz, 14, 47
Avocados
    Rice-and-Bean Tacos with Corn, 131–34
    Steak Tacos, Black Beans, and Chips with Salsa, 49–52
    testing for ripeness, 49
    Turkey, Green Beans, Salad, and Bread, 72–75

B

Bacon
    grease, discarding, 78
    Pork Chops, Green Beans, Salad, and Bread, 77–80
Baker, Chet, *The Best of Chet Baker Sings*, 17, 52, 103
Baking pans, large and small, 4, **4**
Baking sheet, 4, **4**
Balsamic vinegar, 5
Basil
    Chicken-and-Veggie Stir-Fry with Rice, 59–61
    Pasta and Mushrooms, with Salad and Bread, 119–21

    Sole, Mini-Broccoli, Rice, and Toast, 100–103
    Tomato-Basil Pasta, Salad, and Toast, 111–13
Beans
    Beef-Asparagus Stir-Fry with Rice and Soybeans, 37–39
    edamame, 37, 39
    green, buying, 72
    Pork Chops, Green Beans, Salad, and Bread, 77–80
    Rice-and-Bean Tacos with Corn, 131–34
    Shrimp Tacos, Rice, Beans, and Zucchini, 95–98
    Steak, Potatoes, Green Beans, and Salad, 29–31
    Steak Tacos, Black Beans, and Chips with Salsa, 49–52
    Turkey, Green Beans, Salad, and Bread, 72–75
Bean sprouts
    Beef-Asparagus Stir-Fry with Rice and Soybeans, 37–39
    Chicken-and-Veggie Stir-Fry with Rice, 59–61
Beef
    Beef-Asparagus Stir-Fry with Rice and Soybeans, 37–39
    Steak, Potatoes, Green Beans, and Salad, 29–31
    Steak and Potatoes with Spinach and Shrimp, 33–35
    steaks, buying, 29
    Steak Tacos, Black Beans, and Chips with Salsa, 49–52
    Veal with Pasta and Asparagus, 41–43
Bee Gees, *Best of Bee Gees*, 17–18, 75, 121
Beer glasses, 7
Belgian endives, 56
    buying, 29
    Chicken, Veggies, and Salad, 55–57
    Steak, Potatoes, Green Beans, and Salad, 29–31
Beringer Founders' Estate Chardonnay, 16, 43, 93, 103, 121, 125
Berries
    Fresh Strawberries with Sour Cream & Brown Sugar, 138
    Lemon & Berry Sorbet with Fresh Raspberries, 140
    Lemon Tarts with Fresh Blueberries, 139
Blueberries
    Lemon Tarts with Fresh Blueberries, 139
Bonny Doon Big House Red, 14, 108
Bowl(s)
    cereal, 7
    mixing, 4, **4**
    salad, 7
Broccoli
    Chicken-and-Veggie Stir-Fry with Rice, 59–61
    Sole, Mini-Broccoli, Rice, and Toast, 100–103
Bruntell, Peter, *Normal for Bridgewater*, 18, 108, 134
Buckley, Tim, *Happy Sad*, 18, 65
Butter, 5

C

Cabernet Sauvignon
   Cousino Macul Cabernet Sauvignon Antiguas Riserva, 15, 52
   Mountain View Cabernet Sauvignon, 14, 31
Caboodle (Pasta and Mushrooms, with Salad and Bread), 119–21
Cale, John, *Paris 1919*, 18, 108
California wines
   Beringer Founders' Estate Chardonnay, 16, 43, 93, 103, 121, 125
   Bonny Doon Big House Red, 14, 108
   Clos du Bois Merlot, 14, 31
   Mountain View Cabernet Sauvignon, 14, 31
   Ravenswood Zinfandel Vintners Blend, 15, 39, 113
   Ridge Central Coast Zinfandel, 15, 47
Candles, 10
Can opener, 4, 4
Carnophile (Steak, Potatoes, Green Beans, and Salad), 29–31
Carrots
   Chicken, Veggies, and Salad, 55–57
   Chicken-and-Veggie Stir-Fry with Rice, 59–61
Casa Lapostolle Sauvignon Blanc, 16, 57, 65, 75, 129
Cereal bowls, 7
Chardonnay
   Beringer Founders' Estate Chardonnay, 16, 43, 93, 103, 121, 125
   Lindemans Bin 65 Chardonnay, 16, 93, 108, 125
   Louis Jadot Mâcon-Villages, 16, 43, 57, 70, 103, 121
   Louis Latour Mâcon-Lugny, 16, 93, 103, 121, 125
Château Larose-Trintaudon Haut-Médoc, 14, 31
Château Lynch-Bages Pauillac, 15, 35
Cheese
   blue, buying, 55
   Chicken, Couscous, Zucchini, and Salad, 67–70
   Chicken, Veggies, and Salad, 55–57
   Creamy Yellow Rice, Asparagus, Salad, and Bread, 127–29
   feta, 69
   Lamb Chops, Veggies, and Salad, 45–47
   mozzarella, 119
   Parmesan, buying, 41
   Pasta and Mushrooms, with Salad and Bread, 119–21
   Pasta with Veggies, Salad, and Bread, 115–17
   Pork, Cornmeal Mush, and Tomatoes, 63–65
   Pork Chops, Green Beans, Salad, and Bread, 77–80
   Ravioli, Asparagus, and Bread, 123–25
   Salmon, Couscous, Peas, and Salad, 87–89
   Steak, Potatoes, Green Beans, and Salad, 29–31
   Swordfish, Veggies, Potatoes, and Toast, 105–8
   Tomato-Basil Pasta, Salad, and Toast, 111–13
   Veal with Pasta and Asparagus, 41–43
Cheesier (Ravioli, Asparagus, and Bread), 123–25
Chicken
   Chicken, Couscous, Zucchini, and Salad, 67–70
   Chicken, Veggies, and Salad, 55–57
   Chicken-and-Veggie Stir-Fry with Rice, 59–61
Chilean wines
   Casa Lapostolle Sauvignon Blanc, 16, 57, 65, 75, 129
   Cousino Macul Cabernet Sauvignon Antiguas Riserva, 15, 52
Chocolate
   Vanilla Bean Ice Cream with Kahlúa, Hot Fudge, Chocolate-Covered Espresso Beans, & Whipped Cream, 142
Chopping ingredients, **6**, 6
Cilantro
   Rice-and-Bean Tacos with Corn, 131–34
   Shrimp Tacos, Rice, Beans, and Zucchini, 95–98
   Steak Tacos, Black Beans, and Chips with Salsa, 49–52
Clos du Bois Merlot, 14, 31
Cole, Lloyd, *Love Story*, 18, 80
Coltrane, John, *Lush Life*, 18, 47
Conde de Valdemar Crianza Rioja, 14, 65
Conte, Paolo, *The Best of Paolo Conte*, 18–19, 43, 113
Corkscrew/wine opener, 7
Corn
   Rice-and-Bean Tacos with Corn, 131–34
   Steak Tacos, Black Beans, and Chips with Salsa, 49–52
Cornmeal
   polenta, buying, 63
   Pork, Cornmeal Mush, and Tomatoes, 63–65
Couscous
   buying, 67
   Chicken, Couscous, Zucchini, and Salad, 67–70
   Salmon, Couscous, Peas, and Salad, 87–89
Cousino Macul Cabernet Sauvignon Antiguas Riserva, 15, 52
Cucumbers
   buying, 67
   Chicken, Couscous, Zucchini, and Salad, 67–70
   Tuna, Rice, Veggies, and Cucumber Salad, 83–85
Cutting board, 4, 4

D

Davis, Miles, *Porgy and Bess*, 19, 80, 117
Desserts
   Fresh Strawberries with Sour Cream & Brown Sugar, 138
   Lemon & Berry Sorbet with Fresh Raspberries, 140

Lemon Tarts with Fresh Blueberries, 139
Three Flavors of Japanese Mochi Ice Cream, 141
Vanilla Bean Ice Cream with Kahlúa, Hot Fudge, Chocolate-
    Covered Espresso Beans, & Whipped Cream, 142
Warm Apple Tarts with Vanilla Ice Cream, 143
Dicing ingredients, **6**, 6
Dijon mustard, 5
Dill
    Lobster, Asparagus, Potatoes, and Bread, 91–93
    Salmon, Couscous, Peas, and Salad, 87–89
Dishes, washing, 11
Double Shot (Pork Chops, Green Beans, Salad, and Bread),
    77–80
Drake, Nick, *Pink Moon*, 19, 43, 125
Dunnery, Francis, *Man*, 19, 89
Dylan, Bob, *Nashville Skyline*, 19, 57

E

Edamame, 37
    Beef-Asparagus Stir-Fry with Rice and Soybeans, 37–39
    how to eat, 39
Eggs
    Pork Chops, Green Beans, Salad, and Bread, 77–80
Ellington, Duke, and His Orchestra, *. . . And His Mother
    Called Him Bill*, 19, 89
Endives. *See* Belgian endives
Entertaining tips about
    flowers and candles, 10
    greeting guest, 11
    guest's food preferences, 9
    housecleaning, 9–10
    music and lighting, 10
    serving dinner, 11
Equipment, kitchen, 3–5, **3–5**
Evans, Bill, Trio, *Sunday at the Village Vanguard*, 19–20, 35, 85
Everything but the Girl, *Amplified Heart*, 20, 70, 125

F

Falesco Est! Est!! Est!!!, 16, 129
Firesteed Pinot Noir, 14, 80
Fish
    pairing with wines, 13
    Salmon, Couscous, Peas, and Salad, 87–89
    Sole, Mini-Broccoli, Rice, and Toast, 100–103
    Swordfish, Veggies, Potatoes, and Toast, 105–8
    Tuna, Rice, Veggies, and Cucumber Salad, 83–85

Flowers, 10
Foil, aluminum, 5
Forks, for place settings, 7, 7
French red wines
    Château Larose-Trintaudon Haut-Médoc, 14, 31
    Château Lynch-Bages Pauillac, 15, 35
    Guigal Côtes du Rhône, 15, 65
    La Vieille Ferme Côtes du Ventoux, 14, 75
    Louis Jadot Bourgogne Pinot Noir, 15, 75, 80, 85, 89
    M. Chapoutier Crozes-Hermitages *Les Meysonniers*, 15, 43,
        47
French white wines
    Louis Jadot Mâcon-Villages, 16, 43, 57, 70, 103, 121
    Louis Latour Mâcon-Lugny, 16, 93, 103, 121, 125
    Pierre Sparr Gewürztraminer *Carte d'Or*, 16, 61, 85, 98
    Trimbach Pinot Blanc, 16, 80, 85, 89
Frenzy (Swordfish, Veggies, Potatoes, and Toast), 105–8
Fruits. *See* Apples; Berries; Lemons
Frying pans with lid, **3**, 3–4

G

Gainsbourg, Serge, *Couleur Café*, 20, 31, 129
Garlic, 5
German wines
    Joh. Jos. Prüm Riesling Kabinett, 16, 39, 61, 98
Gewürztraminer
    Pierre Sparr Gewürztraminer *Carte d'Or*, 16, 61, 85, 98
Giuffre, Jimmy, 3, *The Jimmy Giuffre 3*, 20, 57, 129
Glasses, 7, 7
Grains. *See* Cornmeal; Rice
Grater, 4, 4
Green beans
    buying, 72
    Pork Chops, Green Beans, Salad, and Bread, 77–80
    Steak, Potatoes, Green Beans, and Salad, 29–31
    Turkey, Green Beans, Salad, and Bread, 72–75
Greens. *See also* Spinach
    Chicken, Couscous, Zucchini, and Salad, 67–70
    Chicken, Veggies, and Salad, 55–57
    Creamy Yellow Rice, Asparagus, Salad, and Bread,
        127–29
    Lamb Chops, Veggies, and Salad, 45–47
    mesclun, buying, 45
    Pasta with Veggies, Salad, and Bread, 115–17
    Salmon, Couscous, Peas, and Salad, 87–89
    Tomato-Basil Pasta, Salad, and Toast, 111–13

Guacamole
    Rice-and-Bean Tacos with Corn, 131–34
    Steak Tacos, Black Beans, and Chips with Salsa, 49–52
Guigal Côtes du Rhône, 15, 65

H

Halstead, Neil, *Sleeping on Roads*, 20, 52, 121
Harmonious (Tuna, Rice, Veggies, and Cucumber Salad),
    83–85
Hawley, Richard, *Late Night Final*, 20, 89, 103
Henry, Joe, *Scar*, 20, 47
Herbage (Chicken, Couscous, Zucchini, and Salad), 67–70
Herbs. *See* Basil; Cilantro; Dill; Rosemary
Hibernation (Chicken, Veggies, and Salad), 55–57
Holiday, Billie, *Lady Day: The Best of Billie Holiday*, 20–21,
    31, 61
Hosting duties, 11
Hot and Bothered (Chicken-and-Veggie Stir-Fry with Rice),
    59–61
Housecleaning tips, 9–10

I

Ice cream
    Three Flavors of Japanese Mochi Ice Cream, 141
    Vanilla Bean Ice Cream with Kahlúa, Hot Fudge,
        Chocolate-Covered Espresso Beans, & Whipped
        Cream, 142
    Warm Apple Tarts with Vanilla Ice Cream, 143
Ingredients
    basic, for recipes, 5
    dicing, **6**, 6
Italian-style dishes
    Creamy Yellow Rice, Asparagus, Salad, and Bread, 127–29
    Pasta and Mushrooms, with Salad and Bread, 119–21
    Pasta with Veggies, Salad, and Bread, 115–17
    Pork, Cornmeal Mush, and Tomatoes, 63–65
    Ravioli, Asparagus, and Bread, 123–25
    Tomato-Basil Pasta, Salad, and Toast, 111–13
    Veal with Pasta and Asparagus, 41–43
Italian wines
    Argiolas Costera, 14, 39, 117
    Falesco Est! Est!! Est!!!, 16, 129
    Piero Antinori Chianti Classico, 15, 108, 113, 117
    S. Quirico Vernaccia di San Gimignano, 16, 57, 70, 129
    Taurino Salice Salentino Riserva, 14, 117
Italicized (Veal with Pasta and Asparagus), 41–43

J

Jackson, Joe, *Night and Day*, 21, 39
Joh. Jos. Prüm Riesling Kabinett, 16, 39, 61, 98

K

Killa (Salmon, Couscous, Peas, and Salad), 87–89
Kitchen equipment, 3–5, **3–5**
Knives, for
    cooking, 4, **4**
    place settings, 7, **7**

L

Lamb
    Lamb Chops, Veggies, and Salad, 45–47
Lane, Ronnie, and Slim Chance, *Anymore for Anymore*, 21, 117
La Vieille Ferme Côtes du Ventoux, 14, 75
Left Banke, The, *There's Gonna Be a Storm*, 21, 75
Lemons
    Lemon & Berry Sorbet with Fresh Raspberries, 140
    Lemon Tarts with Fresh Blueberries, 139
Lights and candles, 10
Lindemans Bin 65 Chardonnay, 16, 93, 108, 125
Lip Smacker (Pasta with Veggies, Salad, and Bread), 115–17
Lobster
    Lobster, Asparagus, Potatoes, and Bread, 91–93
Lotto (Creamy Yellow Rice, Asparagus, Salad, and Bread), 127–29
Louis Jadot Bourgogne Pinot Noir, 15, 75, 80, 85, 89
Louis Jadot Mâcon-Villages, 16, 43, 57, 70, 103, 121
Louis Latour Mâcon-Lugny, 16, 93, 103, 121, 125

M

M. Chapoutier Crozes-Hermitages *Les Meysonniers*, 15, 43, 47
Malbec
    Navarro Correas Malbec, 15, 113
    Trapiche "Oak Cask" Malbec, 14, 35
Massive Attack, *Blue Lines*, 21, 61, 121
Mazzy Star, *So Tonight That I Might See*, 21–22, 35, 98
Measuring cups and spoons, 4, **4**
Meat thermometer, 5, **5**
Mediterranean-style dishes
    Chicken, Couscous, Zucchini, and Salad, 67–70
    Swordfish, Veggies, Potatoes, and Toast, 105–8
Merlot
    Clos du Bois Merlot, 14, 31
    Weinert Merlot, 15, 35
Mexerciser (Rice-and-Bean Tacos with Corn), 131–34

Mingus, Charles, *Mingus Ah Um*, 22, 98
Mixing bowls, 4, **4**
Monk, Thelonious, *Thelonius Alone in San Francisco*, 22, 70, 93
Morrison, Van, *Astral Weeks*, 22, 47, 57
Motian, Paul, *Paul Motian on Broadway*, *Vol. 1-3*, 22, 103
Mountain View Cabernet Sauvignon, 14, 31
Mucho (Shrimp Tacos, Rice, Beans, and Zucchini), 95–98
Mushrooms
    buying, 91
    Chicken-and-Veggie Stir-Fry with Rice, 59–61
    Lobster, Asparagus, Potatoes, and Bread, 91–93
    Pasta and Mushrooms, with Salad and Bread, 119–21
    Pasta with Veggies, Salad, and Bread, 115–17
    Pork Chops, Green Beans, Salad, and Bread, 77–80
    Tuna, Rice, Veggies, and Cucumber Salad, 83–85
    wild, buying, 119
Music
    recommended CDs, 17–25
    volume for, 10
Mustard, Dijon, 5

N

Napkins, 7, **7**
Nascimento, Milton, and Lô Borges, *Clube Da Esquina*, 22, 85
Navarro Correas Malbec, 15, 113
N'Dour, Youssou, *Guide (Wommat)*, 22–23, 61, 134
Nelson, Willie, *Red Headed Stranger*, 23, 98, 125
No-meat dishes
    Creamy Yellow Rice, Asparagus, Salad, and Bread, 127–29
    Pasta and Mushrooms, with Salad and Bread, 119–21
    Pasta with Veggies, Salad, and Bread, 115–17
    Ravioli, Asparagus, and Bread, 123–25
    Rice-and-Bean Tacos with Corn, 131–34
    Tomato-Basil Pasta, Salad, and Toast, 111–13
Nuts
    Pasta with Veggies, Salad, and Bread, 115–17
    Steak, Potatoes, Green Beans, and Salad, 29–31

O

Oil, 5
Olive oil, extra virgin, 5
Onions, dicing, **6**, 6
Oregon wines
    Adelsheim Pinot Gris, 16, 70, 89
    Firesteed Pinot Noir, 14, 80
Orton, Beth, *Central Reservation*, 23, 43, 129

P

Paper towels, 5, **5**
Parsnips
    buying, 55
    Chicken, Veggies, and Salad, 55–57
Pass, Joe, *Virtuoso*, 23, 52
Pasta. *See also* Couscous
    fresh ravioli, buying, 123
    Pasta and Mushrooms, with Salad and Bread, 119–21
    Pasta with Veggies, Salad, and Bread, 115–17
    Ravioli, Asparagus, and Bread, 123–25
    Tomato-Basil Pasta, Salad, and Toast, 111–13
    Veal with Pasta and Asparagus, 41–43
Peas
    Lamb Chops, Veggies, and Salad, 45–47
    Salmon, Couscous, Peas, and Salad, 87–89
Peeler, vegetable, 4, **4**
Pepper, white, 5
Peppercorns, black, 5, 33, 45
Pepper mill, 4, **4**
Peppers
    Chicken-and-Veggie Stir-Fry with Rice, 59–61
    Steak Tacos, Black Beans, and Chips with Salsa,
        49–52
    Swordfish, Veggies, Potatoes, and Toast, 105–8
Pernice Brothers, The, *Overcome by Happiness*, 23, 93
Pesto
    Pork, Cornmeal Mush, and Tomatoes, 63–65
    Tomato-Basil Pasta, Salad, and Toast, 111–13
Piero Antinori Chianti Classico, 15, 108, 113, 117
Pierre Sparr Gewürztraminer *Carte d'Or*, 16, 61, 85, 98
Pine nuts
    Pasta with Veggies, Salad, and Bread, 115–17
Pinot Blanc
    Trimbach Pinot Blanc, 16, 80, 85, 89
Pinot Gris
    Adelsheim Pinot Gris, 16, 70, 89
Pinot Noir
    Firesteed Pinot Noir, 14, 80
    Louis Jadot Bourgogne Pinot Noir, 15, 75, 80, 85, 89
Place setting, 7
Plastic wrap, 5
Plates, 7, **7**
Polenta
    buying, 63
    Pork, Cornmeal Mush, and Tomatoes, 63–65

Pork
    bacon grease, discarding, 78
    Pork, Cornmeal Mush, and Tomatoes, 63–65
    Pork Chops, Green Beans, Salad, and Bread, 77–80
    prosciutto, 41
    Veal with Pasta and Asparagus, 41–43
Potatoes
    Chicken, Veggies, and Salad, 55–57
    Lobster, Asparagus, Potatoes, and Bread, 91–93
    Steak, Potatoes, Green Beans, and Salad, 29–31
    Steak and Potatoes with Spinach and Shrimp, 33–35
    Swordfish, Veggies, Potatoes, and Toast, 105–8
Pot holders, 5, **5**
Poultry
    Chicken, Couscous, Zucchini, and Salad, 67–70
    Chicken, Veggies, and Salad, 55–57
    Chicken-and-Veggie Stir-Fry with Rice, 59–61
    Turkey, Green Beans, Salad, and Bread, 72–75
Prekop, Sam, *Sam Prekop*, 23, 31, 113
Prosciutto, 41
    Veal with Pasta and Asparagus, 41–43

R

Radicchio
    buying, 111
    Tomato-Basil Pasta, Salad, and Toast, 111–13
Raspberries
    Lemon & Berry Sorbet with Fresh Raspberries, 140
Ravenswood Zinfandel Vintners Blend, 15, 39, 113
Ravioli
    fresh, buying, 123
    Ravioli, Asparagus, and Bread, 123–25
Red meat dishes
    Beef-Asparagus Stir-Fry with Rice and Soybeans, 37–39
    Lamb Chops, Veggies, and Salad, 45–47
    pairing with wines, 13
    Steak, Potatoes, Green Beans, and Salad, 29–31
    Steak and Potatoes with Spinach and Shrimp, 33–35
    Steak Tacos, Black Beans, and Chips with Salsa, 49–52
    Veal with Pasta and Asparagus, 41–43
Red wines, recommended, 14–15
Red wine vinegar, 5
Rice
    Beef-Asparagus Stir-Fry with Rice and Soybeans, 37–39
    Chicken-and-Veggie Stir-Fry with Rice, 59–61
    Creamy Yellow Rice, Asparagus, Salad, and Bread, 127–29

long-grain, 95
    Rice-and-Bean Tacos with Corn, 131–34
    Shrimp Tacos, Rice, Beans, and Zucchini, 95–98
    Sole, Mini-Broccoli, Rice, and Toast, 100–103
    Tuna, Rice, Veggies, and Cucumber Salad, 83–85
Ridge Central Coast Zinfandel, 15, 47
Riesling
    Joh. Jos. Prüm Riesling Kabinett, 16, 39, 61, 98
Rock Star (Lamb Chops, Veggies, and Salad), 45–47
Rosemary
    buying, 63
    Chicken, Veggies, and Salad, 55–57
    Lamb Chops, Veggies, and Salad, 45–47
    Pork, Cornmeal Mush, and Tomatoes, 63–65
Roxy Music, *Avalon*, 23, 85
Rustic (Tomato-Basil Pasta, Salad, and Toast), 111–13

S

S. Quirico Vernaccia di San Gimignano, 16, 57, 70, 129
Saffron, 95
    Creamy Yellow Rice, Asparagus, Salad, and Bread, 127–29
    Shrimp Tacos, Rice, Beans, and Zucchini, 95–98
Salad bowl, 7
Salads
    Chicken, Couscous, Zucchini, and Salad, 67–70
    Chicken, Veggies, and Salad, 55–57
    Creamy Yellow Rice, Asparagus, Salad, and Bread, 127–29
    Lamb Chops, Veggies, and Salad, 45–47
    Pasta and Mushrooms, with Salad and Bread, 119–21
    Pasta with Veggies, Salad, and Bread, 115–17
    Pork Chops, Green Beans, Salad, and Bread, 77–80
    Ravioli, Asparagus, and Bread, 123–25
    Salmon, Couscous, Peas, and Salad, 87–89
    Steak, Potatoes, Green Beans, and Salad, 29–31
    Tomato-Basil Pasta, Salad, and Toast, 111–13
    Tuna, Rice, Veggies, and Cucumber Salad, 83–85
    Turkey, Green Beans, Salad, and Bread, 72–75
    Veal with Pasta and Asparagus, 41–43
Salmon
    Salmon, Couscous, Peas, and Salad, 87–89
Salsa
    Rice-and-Bean Tacos with Corn, 131–34
    Shrimp Tacos, Rice, Beans, and Zucchini, 95–98
    Steak Tacos, Black Beans, and Chips with Salsa, 49–52
Salt, 5
Saucepans, 3, **3**

Saucy (Sole, Mini-Broccoli, Rice, and Toast), 100–103
Sauvignon Blanc
    Casa Lapostolle Sauvignon Blanc, 16, 57, 65, 75, 129
Scissors, kitchen, 4, **4**
Seafood. *See* Fish; Sea meat dishes; Shellfish
Sea meat dishes
    Lobster, Asparagus, Potatoes, and Bread, 91–93
    Salmon, Couscous, Peas, and Salad, 87–89
    Shrimp Tacos, Rice, Beans, and Zucchini, 95–98
    Sole, Mini-Broccoli, Rice, and Toast, 100–103
    Swordfish, Veggies, Potatoes, and Toast, 105–8
    Tuna, Rice, Veggies, and Cucumber Salad, 83–85
Serving spoons, 7
Sesame oil, toasted, 5
Sesame seeds
    Chicken-and-Veggie Stir-Fry with Rice, 59–61
    Tuna, Rice, Veggies, and Cucumber Salad, 83–85
Shellfish
    Lobster, Asparagus, Potatoes, and Bread, 91–93
    pairing with wines, 13
    Shrimp Tacos, Rice, Beans, and Zucchini, 95–98
    Steak and Potatoes with Spinach and Shrimp, 33–35
Shrimp
    Shrimp Tacos, Rice, Beans, and Zucchini, 95–98
    Steak and Potatoes with Spinach and Shrimp, 33–35
Sole
    Sole, Mini-Broccoli, Rice, and Toast, 100–103
Sorbet
    Lemon & Berry Sorbet with Fresh Raspberries, 140
Southwestern-style dishes
    Rice-and-Bean Tacos with Corn, 131–34
    Shrimp Tacos, Rice, Beans, and Zucchini, 95–98
    Steak Tacos, Black Beans, and Chips with Salsa, 49–52
Soybeans. *See* Edamame
Soy sauce, 5, 37
Spanish wines
    Conde de Valdemar Crianza Rioja, 14, 65
Spatula, 4, **4**
Spinach
    Pasta with Veggies, Salad, and Bread, 115–17
    Pork Chops, Green Beans, Salad, and Bread, 77–80
    Steak and Potatoes with Spinach and Shrimp, 33–35
    washing, 115
Spoons
    measuring, 4, **4**
    for place settings, 7, **7**

serving, 7
    wooden, 4, **4**
Squash
    Chicken, Couscous, Zucchini, and Salad, 67–70
    Shrimp Tacos, Rice, Beans, and Zucchini, 95–98
    Swordfish, Veggies, Potatoes, and Toast, 105–8
Sticky (Beef-Asparagus Stir-Fry with Rice and Soybeans),
    37–39
Stir-fries
    Beef-Asparagus Stir-Fry with Rice and Soybeans, 37–39
    Chicken-and-Veggie Stir-Fry with Rice, 59–61
    Tuna, Rice, Veggies, and Cucumber Salad, 83–85
Stockpot with lid, 3, **3**
Strainer, 4, **4**
Strawberries
    Fresh Strawberries with Sour Cream & Brown Sugar,
    138
Swagger (Steak Tacos, Black Beans, and Chips with Salsa),
    49–52
Swordfish
    Swordfish, Veggies, Potatoes, and Toast, 105–8
Syrah
    M. Chapoutier Crozes-Hermitages *Les Meysonniers*, 15, 43,
    47
    Wyndham Estates Bin 555 Shiraz, 14, 47

T

Tacos
    Rice-and-Bean Tacos with Corn, 131–34
    Shrimp Tacos, Rice, Beans, and Zucchini, 95–98
    Steak Tacos, Black Beans, and Chips with Salsa, 49–52
Tag Team (Steak and Potatoes with Spinach and Shrimp),
    33–35
Talk Talk, *The Colour of Spring*, 24, 70, 113
Tarts
    Lemon Tarts with Fresh Blueberries, 139
    Warm Apple Tarts with Vanilla Ice Cream, 143
Tatum, Art, *The Art Tatum Solo Masterpieces, Vol. 4*, 24, 39
Taurino Salice Salentino Riserva, 14, 117
Tender (Pork, Cornmeal Mush, and Tomatoes), 63–65
Tequila, 49
Thermometer, meat, 5, **5**
Timer, 5, **5**
Titillated (Lobster, Asparagus, Potatoes, and Bread),
    91–93
Toasted sesame oil, 5

Tomatoes
Chicken, Couscous, Zucchini, and Salad, 67–70
Creamy Yellow Rice, Asparagus, Salad, and Bread, 127–29
Pasta and Mushrooms, with Salad and Bread, 119–21
Pasta with Veggies, Salad, and Bread, 115–17
Pork, Cornmeal Mush, and Tomatoes, 63–65
Rice-and-Bean Tacos with Corn, 131–34
Salmon, Couscous, Peas, and Salad, 87–89
Shrimp Tacos, Rice, Beans, and Zucchini, 95–98
Sole, Mini-Broccoli, Rice, and Toast, 100–103
Steak Tacos, Black Beans, and Chips with Salsa, 49–52
Swordfish, Veggies, Potatoes, and Toast, 105–8
Tomato-Basil Pasta, Salad, and Toast, 111–13
Turkey, Green Beans, Salad, and Bread, 72–75
Tongs, 4, **4**
Tortillas
Rice-and-Bean Tacos with Corn, 131–34
Shrimp Tacos, Rice, Beans, and Zucchini, 95–98
Steak Tacos, Black Beans, and Chips with Salsa, 49–52
Trapiche "Oak Cask" Malbec, 14, 35
Trimbach Pinot Blanc, 16, 80, 85, 89
Tuna
Tuna, Rice, Veggies, and Cucumber Salad, 83–85
Turkey
Turkey, Green Beans, Salad, and Bread, 72–75
Tyrell's Long Flat Red, 14, 52

U

Utensils, eating and drinking, 7, **7**

V

Various Artists, *Brazil Classics 1: Beleza Tropical*, 24, 65
Vaughan, Sarah, *After Hours*, 24, 35
Veal
Veal with Pasta and Asparagus, 41–43
Vegetable peeler, 4, **4**
Vegetables. *See specific vegetables*
Velvet Underground, The, *Loaded*, 24
Vibrations (Turkey, Green Beans, Salad, and Bread), 72–75
Vinegar, 5

W

Waits, Tom, *Closing Time*, 24, 80, 117
Walnuts
Steak, Potatoes, Green Beans, and Salad, 29–31

Watercress
Chicken, Veggies, and Salad, 55–57
Water glasses, 7, **7**
Weinert Merlot, 15, 35
Weller, Paul, *Paul Weller*, 24–25, 65
Whisk, 4, **4**
White meat dishes
Chicken, Couscous, Zucchini, and Salad, 67–70
Chicken, Veggies, and Salad, 55–57
Chicken-and-Veggie Stir-Fry with Rice, 59–61
pairing with wines, 13
Pork, Cornmeal Mush, and Tomatoes, 63–65
Pork Chops, Green Beans, Salad, and Bread, 77–80
Turkey, Green Beans, Salad, and Bread, 72–75
White wines, recommended, 16
Wines, 13–16
geographical regions of, 13
glasses for, 7, **7**
labels on, 13
pairing with foods, 13
red, 14–15
serving temperature for, 13
types of grapes for, 13
white, 16
wine opener/corkscrew for, 7
Wooden spoon, 4, **4**
Wyndham Estates Bin 555 Shiraz, 14, 47

Y

Yams
buying, 45
Lamb Chops, Veggies, and Salad, 45–47

Z

Zero 7, *Simple Things*, 25, 39, 134
Zinfandel
Ravenswood Zinfandel Vintners Blend, 15, 39, 113
Ridge Central Coast Zinfandel, 15, 47
Zombies, The, *Odyssey & Oracle*, 25, 108
Zucchini
Chicken, Couscous, Zucchini, and Salad, 67–70
Shrimp Tacos, Rice, Beans, and Zucchini, 95–98
Swordfish, Veggies, Potatoes, and Toast, 105–8